Answering Teens' Tough Questions

mk Eagle

Neal-Schuman
An imprint of the American Library Association
Chicago 2012

Published in cooperation with the Young Adult Library Services Association.

Printed in the United States of America
16 15 14 13 12   5 4 3 2 1

Extensive effort has gone into ensuring the reliability of the information in this book; however, the publisher makes no warranty, express or implied, with respect to the material contained herein.

ISBNs: 978-1-55570-794-1 (paper); 978-1-55570-852-8 (PDF); 978-1-55570-854-2 (ePub); 978-1-55570-853-5 (Kindle)

Library of Congress Cataloging-in-Publication Data
Eagle, mk, 1983–
    Answering teens' tough questions : a YALSA guide / mk Eagle.
      p. cm.
    Includes bibliographical references and index.
    ISBN 978-1-55570-794-1
    1. Libraries and teenagers—United States. 2. Young adults' libraries—United States. 3. Young adult services librarians—United States—Attitudes. 4. Teenagers—United States—Attitudes. 5. Teenagers—United States—Social conditions. 6. Teenagers—Services for—United States. I. Young Adult Library Services Association. II. Title.

Z718.5.E19 2012
027.62'6—dc23

                                                                          2012015104

Cover design by Rosemary Holderby, Cole Design & Production
Text design in Bodoni and Univers Condensed by UB Communications

♾ This paper meets the requirements of ANSI/NISO Z39.48-1992 (Permanence of Paper).

Contents

Foreword

In the past ten years, I have done more than 100 workshops around the country about working with teens in a library setting. The comment I hear most often from workshop attendees is that they want to do right by the teens in their library, but they have no formal training about working with adolescents. The idea for the YALSA Guides series came about when I realized that what these librarians and frontline staff need are simple, practical guidebooks about best practices for working with teens. Since no one does professional development and opportunities for growth better than the Young Adult Library Services Association (YALSA), it seemed like a no-brainer to partner with this national association of librarians, library workers, and advocates whose mission is to expand and strengthen library services for teens and some of the best practitioners in the field today. The book you are now holding is one of three inaugural titles in the YALSA Guides series, aka boot camp-in-a-book for library staff new to teen services. In fact, the author of this book, mk Eagle, actually came up with that term to help define this series of books that were developed specifically to help library staff learn the basics about serving teens in libraries.

If you're already familiar with YALSA, you might recognize mk Eagle's name from the *YALSA Blog*. As the *YALSA Blog* manager, mk has been at the forefront of sharing information with teen librarians since 2009. She is also a high school librarian in Massachusetts. Both of these gigs have given mk a unique perspective on both directly serving teens and working with adults who work with teens, and nowhere is that experience more apparent than in this book. Using real-life examples and practical strategies for handling teen life scenarios, mk has created a primer for library staff to guide them in talking with teens about tough and often controversial topics, including sex and sexuality, homelessness, tattoos and piercings, violence in relationships, alcohol and drug use and abuse, mental and emotional health, teen violence and juvenile justice, and technology-related issues. In addition to an overview of each of these topics, mk has included information about adolescent development and the developmental needs of young people, as well as recommendations for empowering teens. All of these elements together create an excellent reference and resource guide to keep librarians who serve teens moving forward in their professional development.

Michele Gorman
Author, *Connecting Young Adults and Libraries: A How-To-Do-It Manual*
Teen Services Coordinator, Charlotte Mecklenburg Library
Editor, Teens at the Library Series

Preface

Your day in the library includes several disturbing images that you think about after you go home:

- One girl was shaking, near tears, trying to get help for her friend who had punched her locker, but she's convinced the nurse won't give her an ace bandage.
- Four older boys surround a slight fourteen-year-old boy, not quite touching him, explaining exactly how they're going to kick his ass after school.
- A boy is convinced that information in books and on the web never quite holds the entire truth, so he wants to know whether you can get AIDS from oral sex.

Working with teens is a roller-coaster ride. No amount of research or theory can prepare you for the reality of daily life with young adults. Sure, you can get instruction on how to effectively manage your space, or how to collaborate with coworkers and market your library's programs. You can keep up with the latest young adult (YA) titles and learn any number of Web 2.0 tools. But when you're actually there, face-to-face with a teen, the game changes.

Librarians who never intended to work with young adults may have no idea what to do the first time a teen asks a question beyond books and databases. Even those of us who trained specifically to work with youth find ourselves stumped, time and again, by questions we never could have anticipated. Increasingly we find ourselves called upon to be social workers, triage nurses, and mediators, answering questions no one prepared us for in library school. I don't know about you, but I'm not in the habit of saying, *"That's not my job."* So what should we do?

Librarians who work with teens have to be prepared for teens to change the game. They're going to ask us questions—deep questions, silly questions, terrifying questions, perplexing questions—and the way we answer may determine the kinds of relationships we're able to have with them. Will we merely be seen as the purveyors of books and databases, or will we be adults who care and can help, even when we're confused, too?

Teens who love historical fiction don't need a librarian who can point to every single historical novel. They don't even need a librarian who *likes* historical fiction.

They need a librarian who can help them find the books they want, and the books they didn't even know they wanted. The same is true in every area of teen services.

Whether you work in a school library or a public library, teens will come to you from all walks of life. They may be in their fourth foster home in as many years. They may be trying to get into Harvard. They may be staying at the library late into the night because their neighborhood isn't safe. They may be scared to tell anyone about a pregnancy. As a librarian, your role is unique. You're not a parent, not a teacher, not a police officer. You don't need to understand their crises on a personal level, but you do need to understand the underlying issues in order to serve your teens well.

Answering Teens' Tough Questions: A YALSA Guide is designed to give you a basic understanding of some of the issues teens today face so that you can know how best to proceed when your young patrons bring those issues into the library. Combining relevant research with practical tips and approaches to real-world scenarios, the chapters that follow will give you a foundation for approaching even the toughest conversations with teens.

After a brief look at personal background and biases as well as discussion of the basic developmental needs of teens, each of the following chapters focuses on one of eight topics:

1. sex and sexuality;
2. homelessness;
3. body modification;
4. dating violence and abuse;
5. drugs and alcohol;
6. mental and emotional health;
7. violence and juvenile justice; and
8. teens and technology.

I would encourage you to turn to the individual chapters when trying to help a teen with a specific problem.

Read collectively, the chapters in *Answering Teens' Tough Questions: A YALSA Guide* are designed to provide a librarian in any setting with the tools to approach virtually any tricky conversation with a teen. By combining summaries of the risks teens face in these eight areas with practical advice and tools for collection development, collaboration, and marketing, this book goes beyond educational theory into the realities of modern teen services.

1

Who Are You, Anyway?—
Your Own Background and Biases

Who You Are

Before we get into teens and who they are, let's talk for a moment about who *you* are. If you're reading this book, you're probably a librarian (or a librarian in training). Beyond that, all bets are off. You might be black, white, Latina, biracial. You could be fresh out of grad school or thirty years into your career. You might be gay, nearsighted, left-handed, agnostic, or a diehard Red Sox fan. Take a minute to think of all the adjectives that could be used to describe you. Go ahead—I'll wait.

Quite a list, isn't it? And there's an important distinction between *ways to describe you* and *ways to describe yourself*. When others see you, or look at your résumé, or sit next to you on the bus, who are they seeing? Can they tell that you're on your way to work? Are they noticing your tattoos or whether your nails are manicured? Do you look friendly, or shy, or scary? Do you sound like you're from around here?

Sometimes the parts of you that you think about the least (consciously, anyway) are the first things strangers notice. Particularly in situations where they might feel vulnerable—late at night, in a deserted subway car, in line at the airport—other people, whether they realize it or not, are making snap judgments about whether you can be trusted, whether you might be dangerous, whether they should keep an eye on you. While they're often targets themselves of this kind of profiling, teens are making these same judgments every time they see you at the library.

Teens are perhaps the masters of quickly assessing the world around them. Whether it's navigating the ever-shifting tides of popularity, gauging what teachers and parents and coaches expect of them, making a split-second decision on a field or court, or just walking home at night, teens are constantly evaluating their environment—an environment that includes you.

One of the panicky thoughts that can surface when we're confronted with a teen's tough question is, *I have no idea what they're going through*. It's not that we don't remember what it's like to be a teenager; as much as we may like to forget some of the more painful memories of adolescence, we were all there once. It's that we simply may not know what it's like to be 15 and pregnant, or black and hassled by the police, or gay and living on the street. How do we overcome these potentially vast chasms of experience to find empathy and positive solutions? And how do we ensure that we work *with* our teens, many of whom have backgrounds so disparate from our own, without claiming to speak *for* them?

First, it's important to take a good, hard look at your own identity and beliefs, as well as the way you express them. Just as shared experiences and outlooks can help you bond with teens, a lack of common ground—or even merely *perceived* differences—can alienate teens. Following are just a few facets of your identity that may impact your authenticity and approachability for the teens you serve.

Gender

No matter your skill and experience in traditional library services or even your rapport with teens, your gender may mean that certain conversations are off limits. Teens grappling with issues related to sex or sexuality in particular may be hesitant to approach anyone but a same-gender adult. This isn't just a case of avoiding cooties; teens have very good reasons to be cautious when it comes to sex and body image. Girls have been socialized to be wary of older men (and men in education and other youth-oriented fields have learned to keep their distance). Boys, on the other hand, face pressure to interpret all interactions with women as sexual—meaning they may face teasing and allegations of romantic interest just for talking or spending too much time with any girl or woman. And some of their concerns should ring true to us as adults. Many women prefer to see female gynecologists, after all, and many men would prefer to discuss concerns such as sexually transmitted infections (STIs) with another man.

Even if the topic of conversation isn't explicitly sexual, teens may make assumptions about your interests or expertise based on your gender. Whether based on tired stereotypes or the day-to-day experiences of teens among their peers, these assumptions can keep some teens from even approaching you. So how can you make yourself available to those teens who don't share your gender identity? Start by treating all your teen patrons as equals. None of us wants to think we're favoring (or shunning) a particular group of teens, but be honest with yourself: do you give some teens more attention? Maybe boys or girls just seem to "naturally" gravitate toward you, but if you're only reaching out to the teens who are already drawn to you, you're missing a lot of teens.

Race

Again, teens may make a lot of (wrong) assumptions about you based on a look—plenty of Latinos and biracial or multiracial folks can pass (and, consequently, be dismissed) as white. On the other hand, being black or Latino doesn't mean that you grew up in the inner city or know anything about hip-hop. The key to connecting across racial lines is authenticity. Teens who balk at confiding in you based on your perceived racial differences will walk away altogether if you try to bluff your way through racially charged conversations.

Authenticity means knowing your community. Are most of your teens staying in school? Do a lot of them work to help support their families? Are some of them already parents? Is crime a major issue? If you know the answers to these questions before you even get to work, you won't be caught flat-footed when a teen brings one of these issues up in conversation—and you won't assume that your teens are all dealing with heavy issues when they're not.

Age

Take a minute to get comfortable with this: You're old. Seriously, you're ancient. You know how you feel when you see a teen's birth date? Yeah, *that* old. Even if only a few years separate you from your teen patrons, to them, you're officially an *Older Person*. And if you can reach back through the cobwebs to remember your younger years, you'll probably recall that it was often hard to reach out to older people when you were a teen. Beyond the standard teen angst of believing that no one could possibly understand, teens have good reason to be wary of confiding in adults. Many adults treat teens like they're still much younger children. Others assume all teens are reckless and dangerous. It's up to you to show your teens that age doesn't have to have anything to do with how well you listen and how supportive you can be.

That said, it's also important for you to not get defensive about your age and play younger. Teens don't really care if you're into Justin Bieber, or texting, or whatever it is you think the kids like these days. You'll probably come off as a little fake if you act like you have *So! Much! In! Common!* with your teen patrons. When it comes to working with teens, the age difference between you will only get in the way if you pretend it isn't there.

Sexuality

If you're visibly LGBTQ (lesbian, gay, bisexual, transgender, or queer) (or perceived as queer), some teens, sadly, will never get close to you. (It might be contagious, after all.) Reputation is crucial in adolescence, and the consequences of hanging out with a queer adult—from peers, teammates, and family members—can be dire. Teens who are questioning their own sexuality may see a little too much of themselves in you and not know how to handle it. All that aside, you're doing incredibly important work by being out and visible. Teens today arguably have many more role models than those of us who grew up before Ellen came out, but it's still very important for teens to have *real* role models in their lives—adults they can talk to and interact with on a personal level, who show them that happiness and success is attainable even if you're not a celebrity.

On the flip side, if you're straight, your queer and questioning teens will scrutinize you as a matter of survival. They will watch and listen carefully before they even speak to you, trying to determine whether or not you can be trusted. Little things that you might not even think about—if you mention LGBTQ plotlines when recommending books, whether or not you tolerate casual homophobic speech, if you've ever mentioned having a gay friend or relative—are the cues that queer teens use to decide whether they can be out and honest with you, or hide like they must from so many other adults.

Religion

Your own religion may have implications for queer teens, but also for teens who are themselves religious or questioning faith. Do you wear overtly religious accessories or clothing? Do you speak openly of God or another deity (or the lack thereof)? Expect frank questions from teens, but also know that your outward displays may leave some cold. On the other hand, especially if you're working outside a school setting (religious displays tending to be kind of *verboten* in public schools and all), you could be the first openly religious adult (or the first openly religious adult from a particular faith) a teen has ever met. This could be a great opportunity to explain faith (or atheism) in a safe, neutral space such as the library, rather than the politically charged atmosphere of the mass media.

It's also important to remember that your religious teens (or teens living in a religious household, which is a crucial distinction) may have needs that are unfamiliar to you, like a desire for "clean" reads. When teens confide that their parents or guardians won't allow them to read certain kinds of books, your gut reaction might be to sneak them the titles anyway. While it's important to defend teens' right to read whatever they choose, sometimes teens tell you about these kinds of parental restrictions *because they want to follow them.* If your library's neighborhood is home to a particular religious community, it's important for you to understand the unique needs of that population so that requests like this won't stump you.

Politics

It's not really anyone's business how you vote or which causes you support, but teens are still going to ask—particularly around election days and whenever an issue or controversy takes over the local news. Remember that although many teens' political views come directly from their parents or other family members, during the teen years—particularly as older teens reach voting age and gain more civic opportunities—teens are forming their *own* identities, and may actively seek out the opinions of other adults outside their families. While it's not okay to recruit at the library (we seek political balance in our programs and collections, after all), it *is* okay to show teens you're passionate about your beliefs.

That said, the teens whose parents won't let them read about vampires or are concerned about too much of a pro-choice bent in news coverage might not get along super well with your "My Body, My Choice" bumper sticker. Recognize that you have every right to your beliefs, and to shout them from the rooftops—but all that shouting might just scare away some teens.

Examining Privilege

Once you've taken stock of the ways you and your teen patrons may or may not find common ground, the next vital step is examining your own privilege. The concept of "the privileged" often brings to mind an image of the well-to-do, or legacy admissions at universities, but privilege is more than just wealth or class. Privilege refers to the ways that certain groups of people enjoy systemic advantages over others. Put another way, it is the way certain identities are understood as "normal," and, by extension, more desirable than those marked as "other" or outside the norm.

"Enjoying" privilege—white privilege, say, or male privilege—doesn't mean nothing bad ever happens to you, of course. You could be a white man and still lose your job, for instance. And being part of a privileged group doesn't always mean you're in the majority. Being part of a privileged group means that *in general*, and historically, your group enjoys certain advantages over other groups—which can have very real implications for you as an individual.

Try asking yourself a few basic questions:

- If I call the police, can I be confident they will respond quickly and respectfully?
- Can I easily find clothes in my size that match the quality others wear?
- Can I legally marry the partner of my choosing?
- Do I feel safe walking alone at night?
- Can I use a public restroom without incident?
- Do I have control over the medications I take and the treatment I receive?

For every "yes" you answer, you enjoy privilege over many. Our lives are full of intersecting identities, which means we experience privilege (and a lack thereof) in intersecting and evolving ways. It's not about determining whether a black man or a disabled woman faces "worse" obstacles in society; it's about recognizing that viewing yourself as "normal"—and not having to think about the possibility of answering those questions with a resounding no—has real implications for everyone else.

So what does that have to do with teens and libraries?

First, it means that you already have one significant advantage over all the teens you serve: you're an adult. Beyond the legal rights and responsibilities of adulthood (which are huge!), being an adult also means other adults take you seriously. The sad truth is that many adults don't like, trust, or respect teens. Teens are loud! They travel in packs! They have poor impulse control! When teens are having trouble communicating with other adults in their lives, you can help act as a bridge, conveying exactly the same information without your emotions being discounted as childish or your experiences dismissed as immature. Conversely, when you talk to teens, it's important not to assume you know best just because you're older. While it's true that teens' minds and bodies are still developing—the following chapter will address precisely the unique needs of adolescents, and some of the obstacles they may face—their experiences and aspirations are real.

Examining your own privilege also means acknowledging and supporting those real experiences. Trying to approach teens as if they're just like you five or ten (or twenty) years ago won't help your teens, and it very well may alienate them from you altogether. Even if a teen seems similar to you demographically, even if you think you're young and totally with it, you can't give advice to your younger self. Teens today are growing up in a very different world. They may not remember ever flying without taking off their shoes at security. They have lived through one of the greatest economic meltdowns our country has ever seen. Major cultural and political milestones that have shaped *our* lives and beliefs exist for teens only as chapters in textbooks. So how can we relate?

We can begin, of course, by studying the issues, as the following chapters will, but we also need to know our teens. Start by listening. This requires you to be accessible, and nonjudgmental. Teens often initiate with smaller stuff to test the waters. Do you pay attention? Do you seem squeamish about some topics? Do you change the subject a lot, or give unsolicited advice? Your responses and attitude in casual conversations have an impact on whether or not teens will come back to you when they need help.

Knowing teens also means respecting their choices, even when they differ from your own. Actions, of course, are in a category of their own, and successful teen librarians will come up with rules and boundaries collaboratively—with input from teens themselves—and communicate (and enforce) those expectations. But teens' thoughts are their own, and, ultimately, what they do outside the library is up to them. Your advice and support should be grounded in their needs and best interests, not your own ideologies or hopes.

So now take a deep breath, shake out all that nervous energy, and imagine yourself face-to-face with a teen who has some tough questions brewing.

In a way, the script for this kind of interaction (if you can even call it a script; trust me, you're going to be doing a lot of ad-libbing) is like a cross between the reference interview and listening to a patron with a complaint. You're going to need to get to the *real* issue—like you would with a patron who asks about medical books and turns out to have a nasty rash on his foot—but you're also going to need to sit back and do a lot of listening. Teens with sensitive subjects on their minds may come to you with very direct results in mind—i.e., *I need to find a doctor*. They may also come to you with far less direction—*I need to talk to somebody*. How do you find the right balance?

Listen

Your first, last, and most important job is to listen. Whether you're the first person a teen has told or the twenty-seventh, *his or her story is important*. It is not less important than cataloging, or checking in books, or answering your phone. Sure, you don't know what a teen has in mind when he or she walks up to you, and, yes, you might already be in the middle of something. But the second you seem like you're too busy, a teen who might be in crisis is likely to walk away.

Listen attentively, but just as you would with a parent demanding to remove a book from the collection, be careful *how* you listen. Smiling and nodding, though they're practically automatic for those of us who want to be good customer servants, can express agreement. Make it clear when you're agreeing, and when you're just staying with the story. Don't interrupt, and don't start multitasking if the conversation didn't begin that way.

Relax

Some of us immediately tense up when we realize a conversation just got capital S *Serious*, and some of us start to panic when a particular topic surfaces. Maybe for you it's sex, or drugs, or going to the police. It doesn't matter *why* the topic makes you panic; it's just important to know that's your reaction, so that you can work on controlling it. The teen in front of you is probably freaking out a little, and watching that play out on *your* face isn't going to help matters at all. If a teen came to you with a tough question, he or she probably thinks you at least know how to help; you hyperventilating is going to shatter that illusion, and the conversation might end then and there.

It's also important for you to relax and stay calm so that *you* can think clearly. The second your adrenaline kicks in, your thinking is going to cloud. You'll be in panic mode, not your usual rational self. If you want to remember all the resources you have for this particular teen—and you *do*—you need to stay calm so that you can bring them all to mind, and to your teen. Remember that this conversation, this moment, probably isn't the make-or-break moment it feels like. This might be the beginning of an intervention, or the start of a much larger conversation, but it's probably not a hostage situation. You don't have to have all the answers in this split second. You just have to start the ball rolling.

Follow Up

Once the moment has passed—no matter how it passed—don't let this be the end of the conversation. You're not bound to confidentiality like doctors or lawyers, so you don't have to be the only one holding whatever knowledge a teen just shared. You do want to respect your teens' privacy, but you also need to remember you're not an island. You can start small by talking to a coworker, or you can go directly to another professional with the expertise you need.

And follow up with the teen. Check in the next day, or the next week. You don't have to directly reference your conversation, but do see how the teen is doing, and make it clear that you were listening, and that you'll listen again.

Why Me?

At this point we should probably talk a little about *why* it's important to intervene with teens, to have the tough conversations that will likely keep you up at night. This book largely focuses on the *what* and the *how*—what issues teens in your community may be facing, and how you can best support them—but the *why* is just as important. Why get involved? Why step outside your comfort zone? Why can't someone else handle it?

For the luckiest teens, there are an awful lot of *someone elses*. They have parents and family members who care about them. They have teachers and coaches who know them well and want them to succeed. But for a lot of teens, those supports just aren't there. And for others, the issue at hand just seems too weighty to bring home. Teens who seek out your advice (whether they know they're asking for help or not) may be more comfortable with you than with another adult in their lives. They may be scared, embarrassed, and feeling alone. If you could be the one to finally convince them to get help, or to show them they're not alone, or just make a tough conversation a little bit easier, why *wouldn't* you? (If the answer is because *you* feel scared, or embarrassed, or just plain unsure—welcome to the world your teens live in every day!)

2

Who Are Those Teens in Your Library?—A Brief Introduction to Teens Themselves

Developmental Assets for Youth

Unless you're a parent or a researcher, you probably don't know much about the developmental needs of adolescents. There's always the occasional trend piece about how much sleep teens should get, and most of us have had the experience of looking on in awe as a teenager puts away yet another cheeseburger or slice of pizza. We're even finally coming to some kind of consensus on how the developing adolescent brain is, well, *developing*. But what does this unique stage of life mean for those of us who work with teens? What do teens really need, and what should we know about their growing brains and bodies?

The Search Institute, a nonprofit, nonsectarian group dedicated to supporting healthy communities for youth (Search Institute, 2011a), has created a list of 40 Developmental Assets® for youth that have become the standard for those working toward positive teen development. In short, these assets represent the "relationships, opportunities, and personal qualities that young people need to avoid risks and to thrive" (Search Institute, 2011b). The entire list is valuable for those who work with youth and want to see them thrive, but there are eight in particular that those new to youth services should know and use to recognize the ways in which adults and communities might hinder teens' progress toward those assets. This chapter will address these eight assets in order, offering a quick assessment of each so that you can gauge your community's and library's effectiveness in fostering these assets.

Support

This one might seem obvious—how can anyone, teen or adult, thrive without support from others? Many teens have rich support systems, made up of family, friends, teachers, community organizations, even groups such as the police and fire department. They

9

have many adults in their lives urging them to pursue their goals—and maintaining that they can achieve these goals—as well as peers who believe that they can do well. Maybe you were one such teen, and that network of support helped you grow into the confident and capable adult you are now. But many teens aren't so lucky.

For all the hype about America's every-kid-gets-a-trophy culture, in many schools and communities teens have never known success. Perhaps a teen has been shuffled from one foster home to another, never enrolling in one school long enough to see a report card. Maybe the neighborhood is dominated by crime, and a teen with multiple relatives in the justice system has no role models succeeding in legal occupations. In thousands of communities around the country, there are teens who have never been told, "You can do it." Is yours one of them?

First, think about the kinds of businesses and organizations in your community. How many of them are youth-oriented? Do you have adult-youth mentoring programs, such as Big Brothers and Big Sisters? Do your city's or town's businesses sponsor youth athletic teams? (Do you even *have* youth athletic teams?) Are there ample child care and preschool facilities, or are families mostly relying on relatives and neighbors? Is there a youth curfew? Do children and teens attend neighborhood schools, or are they bussed far from home?

Then start to think about the way other adults in your community treat teens. Often in areas where teens tend to congregate, such as subway stations or school parking lots, adults seem determined to keep teens away from each other, as if lowering the number of teens automatically makes a spot safer. In the aftermath of a shooting at a restaurant in my neighborhood—a violent incident *not involving teens*—I witnessed transit police telling a group of teens to "break it up" at a train station over a mile away. The teens were doing nothing but talking to one another.

Do teens who walk into stores in your community get closely watched or even followed by store employees? Do groups of teens in restaurants or cafés get hustled out as soon as they've purchased something? Sometimes teens even get harassed in spaces that were supposed to be explicitly theirs, like skate parks.

What about employment? Do teens bag your groceries or tear your ticket at the movies? Communities with jobs for youth—both jobs explicitly reserved for teens, and jobs that teens might apply for side-by-side with adults—are communities that believe teens can be responsible and productive. Conversely, these are communities where teens see their peers succeeding and have reason to believe they could do the same.

The library can have a role in all these areas of youth support—or be yet another place in your community that doesn't support teens. Does your library have a teen space, separate from the adult and children's sections? How old must a teen be to have his or her own library card, and an account separate from prying parental eyes? Libraries are often great at partnering with community organizations to support younger children—offering summer reading incentives, or providing free or reduced-price tickets to children's museums—but don't always make similar efforts for teens.

How do other library employees and adult patrons treat teens in your library? Are they constantly shushing your teens, demanding that they free up computer stations, or trying to "break up" groups of teens? You have the chance to be an adult—possibly the *first* adult—who treats these teens with respect. You may even find a wealth of volunteers in your midst, who never would have asked to help you because they didn't believe they could.

Empowerment

As adults, we often take our abilities for granted. Many of us have been paying our own bills, making our own meals, and holding down our own jobs for years—so long that we might not remember what it was like before we could drive or vote. But teens may be in a very different situation. Especially before reaching the legal driving and voting ages, teens are often hugely dependent on parents and family members—sometimes so dependent that they may not feel they have a voice of their own.

Empowerment for teens means believing their voices and ideas make a difference. It means being able to influence the direction of their own lives and the lives of others. It means contributing, whether that contribution is merely to a family meal or to a larger organization. But in order for teens to feel empowered, they must be part of a community that welcomes them.

Many of the elements that can stifle teens' feelings of support can also hinder their empowerment. In a community where teens cannot contribute—whether that means there are no jobs for youth, or strict curfews are in place, or there is a lack of opportunities for teens to speak at school and community events—teens have no role models for civic participation. Even teens who do take the plunge and try to speak at a community meeting may quickly be shot down by adults.

Does your town meeting or other community government structure allow for youth participation? Is there a youth advisory board to your city council, or some kind of mayoral coalition for youth? Do teens have a chance to be politically active, or are they limited to high school student council? If teens have a chance at employment in your community, do they have a shot at upward mobility? Can they work hard for a promotion, or are entry-level positions (and entry-level positions *only*) reserved for teens?

In many communities with teen-friendly spaces such as skate parks and youth centers, teens were instrumental in creating those spaces. If a teen in your community spearheaded a letter-writing campaign or tried to get a meeting with the city planning commissioner, what would happen? Would your mayor's office send a standard form letter reply as if a child had written in, or would the commissioner laugh that teen right out of the office?

For teens who must rely on others for transportation and money, empowerment may come in smaller victories. A teen without a driver's license or car may still be active as a leader on a sports team, after-school club, or even the library's teen advisory group. Does your community offer extracurricular opportunities for youth? Do they all require extra fees for participation, or do businesses and community groups sponsor teens who otherwise might not be able to pay?

In the library, teens will feel most empowered when they have a space of their own and know they have a hand in shaping it. Your vision of a young adult area in the library may be quite different from the vision of your young adults. Maybe they feel stifled by the quiet elsewhere in the library, and want a space where they can safely have conversations. Maybe they'd like computers that adults can't poach from them. Maybe they need active space, where an impromptu dance session wouldn't be out of line. Have you *asked* your teen patrons what they'd like?

It's also important to listen to teen voices without adults weighing in, although it may be hard to get some adults to be quiet. Many of us have had the experience of a parent dragging his or her son or daughter up to the desk, asking for a book recommendation, and not letting the poor teen get a word in edgewise. Resist the temptation to follow suit and talk only to the parent as if the teen weren't in the room. Make eye contact with the teen. Ask direct questions, even when the parent believes they've already answered. Teens who believe you care about their opinions are that much more likely to believe they have a stake in their own future, even if it's just their future at the library.

Boundaries and Expectations

Many teens may feel like they already have too many boundaries to contend with, but offering teens a world without boundaries and expectations is setting them up for failure in the real world. It's also setting them up for confusion—if they don't know what's expected of them, how do they know whether they'll be successful? It's like assigning an essay with no parameters, then docking points because it wasn't long enough. Boundaries and expectations for teens can refer to specific rules—teens- or adults-only spaces, curfew hours, the amount of time teens must stay in school—but they can also refer to boundaries and expectations in relationships, both with peers and with other adults.

The teens who may have the hardest time with boundaries are those who have already been asked to grow up too fast. For a teen who's been forced to care for younger siblings from an early age or take on a part-time (or full-time) job to support an ailing parent, age restrictions can seem arbitrary. Why is the driving age set at 16 when many teens have been driving tractors or family vehicles for years? What sense does the legal drinking age make for a teen who has been acting as a lookout for drug transactions since age 12? Teens who live in communities where it's not uncommon for a child to go searching for a parent in a bar or pool hall don't see these spaces as adults-only; why should the activities that take place there be any different?

Boundaries are also difficult for teens wherever adults are inconsistent in setting and enforcing those boundaries. In school settings, teens quickly learn which teachers tightly monitor tardy arrivals to class and which are more likely to look the other way. Underage drinkers figure out which bars (and bartenders) card the most frequently, and drivers of all ages know where and when they can ease the accelerator past the speed limit. These judgment calls—quickly learning the parameters of a situation, and exploiting the more lenient authority figures—aren't unique to teens, but teens who never have to face firm boundaries and clearly stated expectations run the risk of growing into adults who can't follow anyone else's rules.

The key part of the equation, then, is clearly stating the expectations. Do teens in your community know exactly what they need to graduate or receive a GED? Are they expecting to be doctors, lawyers, or professional athletes without even knowing how to get into college? Do the adult spaces in your community—bars, 21+ clubs, even R-rated movies at the local theater—post and enforce their age restrictions?

Within the library, boundaries can be crucial in keeping the various populations your library serves happy, both within their own spheres and wherever services may overlap. Is your young adult area teens-only, or may adults browse specific sections or areas during certain hours? Can teens use computers in the adult section, or read books from the children's room? Do you work only in the teen area, or do you wear multiple hats in the library? Teens may not feel comfortable approaching you if you're working outside the teen area, or they may intrude when you're working with other patrons because they see you as "their" librarian.

At this point it's also important to note that the kinds of boundaries teens need include boundaries in relationships. You may think a teen has crossed the line in asking personal questions or bringing up inappropriate conversation topics, but that teen may not see anything inappropriate about adult-youth friendships—or even romantic relationships. If other adults in a teen's life have blurred the lines between platonic and romantic relationships, it's all the more important for you to make your role clear. You are not a friend, or a peer, or a potential romantic partner. You can be *friendly*, but you are not a friend to the teens you serve; you are an adult who works with youth. No matter how closely you work with teens, no matter how much they may admire and rely on you, you must remain professional if you want teens to respect your own boundaries.

Constructive Use of Time

Teens get tired of hearing, "Don't you have anything *better* to do?" But in many of the spheres of their lives, teens are expected to use their time constructively. If you're a school librarian, particularly if you have the mixed blessing of a computer lab in your space, you're probably all too familiar with policing teens' behaviors. In my first year working in a high school library, I spent study hall on most days walking around the computer labs trying to get students off of games and Facebook. In a way, this asset is similar to the previous one; it's about getting teens to recognize the boundaries between productive time and activities and "wasting" time.

Once again, ask yourself if your community is home to any teen-oriented spaces or organizations. When teens don't have space of their own, they end up perpetually in between activities. Some would call this loitering; I'd call it being disenfranchised. Teens who can't play in a recreational sports league, have a leisurely dinner with friends downtown, or congregate at skate parks and arcades are the ones who end up standing around nowhere in particular. They may catch the attention of adults— groups of teenagers are *scary*, after all—and, accused of being up to no good, can end up in confrontations with adults or take their anger at being wrongly accused out on people or property. This isn't to say that every town without a skate park is going to see all its mailboxes trashed, of course; teens with seemingly nothing to do don't all suddenly turn to a life of crime. But being actively engaged in *something*—whether it's athletics, the performing arts, politics, or community service—is much more likely to keep teens from more dangerous pursuits.

What's the job market like for teens in your area? Do they have volunteer opportunities, such as working on local campaigns or helping out at homeless shelters and soup kitchens? Can teens participate in mentoring programs for younger children, or volunteer at after-school homework and tutoring sessions? Do teens have the chance to pursue internships, through either school or community organizations? Can teens contribute meaningfully to their community, or are they forced to the sidelines as adults do all the "important" work?

In your library, do teens have space and resources to spend their time constructively, whether completing their homework or working on an extracurricular project? Much is made of the need for teens to have social space, where they can talk and interact with peers, but it's important to remember that teens need quiet spaces sometimes, too. If teens feel that they can only get schoolwork done or search online for jobs if they're in the quieter adult library spaces, they're not truly being served by the young adult section.

Commitment to Learning

Just as their bodies are developing during adolescence, teens' minds are developing, too, but only if they have positive role models and the resources necessary to foster learning. Most of us think of the school environment when we think of a commitment to learning, but other areas of the community—and other adults who aren't necessarily educators—can be just as crucial.

It's important to expand the concept of "learning" beyond learning in a strict educational setting. The explicit goal of schools is to teach, of course, and arguably the majority of our learning during the formative years comes as a direct result of the educational system. But to truly support teens as lifelong learners, we must recognize that learning can take many forms. Teens learn while they're working at jobs, while they're consuming popular culture, while they're serving their communities, and while they're navigating the confusing waters of romantic relationships. And teens learn best when they are invested in their own education, which often means teens will succeed the most in areas where they have a personal stake. A teen with an aptitude for art may coast along in school, but soar if given the chance to work with a local artist on a mural installation.

Communities with a proven commitment to education will give teens every opportunity to excel at school. Schools with more community support are more likely to succeed at fundraising, see higher parent turnout at open houses and teacher conferences, and retain high-quality teachers who aren't lured elsewhere by higher salaries and more community engagement. But whether they're at blue-ribbon schools or schools on a turnaround plan, teens may struggle if they have other underlying needs that aren't being addressed. What's health care like in your community? How many of your teens are living below the poverty line? Are students getting the support they need in school, or are some slipping through the cracks with unidentified learning or emotional needs?

In the library, is your staff well-acquainted with the teaching and learning standards for your state? If you're working in a public library, do you have a close working relationship with the schools in your area? Do you know when major projects are due, or the dates of state and national standardized testing? Would you be able to connect a teen to a tutor, teacher, or other mentor to help support his or her academic needs? Do you offer learning activities outside the standard school curriculum, particularly in the summer? Teens need to know that the library is home to all kinds of learning.

Positive Values

If teens are to grow into healthy adults, they must strive toward positive overarching values that define themselves as well as the communities to which they belong. These values include traits such as honesty, loyalty, dedication, and resilience. In order for teens to adopt these values, however, their own communities and the adults around them must hold them as well.

As with previous assets, positive values are only possible in a healthy community. Communities struggling with crime and poverty in particular may offer few adult role models who maintain positive values themselves. When teens see criminals as the most "successful" community members around them, they find it difficult to associate positive values with success. Instead, they may begin to value aggression, dishonesty, greed, and even malice. Does your community reward good citizenship? Do criminals see justice? Do local businesses thrive on cooperation with the community, or exploitation of it? Can teens find positive role models within your community, or must they look to less realistic celebrity figureheads?

Within the library, the teen section can be a microcosm of the community. You can set goals and expectations as a library community (one that *includes* youth, rather than dictating to it) and join in the responsibility of enforcing those expectations rather than relying on adult enforcers. You can model positive values in the way you interact with coworkers and supervisors, as well as the way you interact with patrons of all ages.

Social Competencies

In order for teens to be successful, they must learn to peacefully interact with others—peers, teachers, community members, and family. Interpersonal skills may not come easily to some teens, particularly if they are used to hostility or suspicion from adults, but these skills are crucial in learning to navigate the social world.

Communities where violence is common can leave teens with a lack of restraint and few tools to avoid perpetuating violence. Indeed, many teens approach spaces such as the library with the same defensive (or aggressive) mentality that protects them on the streets, turning young adult sections into turf wars. Does your community have a history of violence, particularly youth violence? Are neighborhoods clearly segregated, or is your community culturally diverse? Do adults model skills such as decision making, empathy, and conflict resolution?

In the library, make the young adult section a peaceful one. Be clear that everyone has a right to the space as long as they hold up their responsibilities—respect for people and property, and behavior that follows the agreed-upon guidelines. Do you recognize and quickly address any hate speech or other aggression? Are you meeting the needs of the full variety of cultural groups your library serves? Is your entire staff, including any security or police presence at the library, well trained in de-escalation?

Positive Identity

Teens who believe they can succeed already have a huge leg up on those who have been told over and over that they are doomed to fail. Positive identity goes beyond mere self-esteem to the belief that a teen is part of something larger and worthwhile, which can be a struggle in communities where success is not modeled well by adults.

Again, communities where "success" is tied to violence or crime offer little in the way of positive role models for teens. Teens see that "success" is a result of aggression, money, and physical power, rather than hard work or positive contributions to the community. Who are the role models in your community? Are there organizations tying positive values, such as community service, to athletics or other extracurricular endeavors? Do teens get positive identity messaging in sports, or do coaches push for winning at any cost? Do schools identify promising (even if struggling) students for further opportunities, or promote only a skilled few at the expense of at-risk students?

In the library, teens need to believe they all have equal opportunities and access to materials and staff. Can anyone join your teen advisory group? Who has input on purchasing and programs? Do the same few teens win every contest and challenge? Are all teens treated equally when they break the rules? A dedication to equality and supporting all teens will make your library a place where teens believe in their own success.

References

Search Institute. 2011a. "About Us." Search Institute. Accessed July 4. http://www.search-institute.org/about.

———. 2011b. "What Kids Need: The Building Blocks for Children and Youth." Search Institute. Accessed July 4. http://www.search-institute.org/developmental-assets.

3

"What If I Go All the Way?"—
Sex and Sexuality

The Data

According to the Centers for Disease Control and Prevention, teen birthrates fell to their lowest rate in U.S. history in 2009, at 39.1 per 1,000 young women, but the United States still tops other industrialized nations, with teen birthrates far above countries like the United Kingdom, Canada, Japan, and the Netherlands (Centers for Disease Control and Prevention, 2011). Eighty-two percent of teen pregnancies are unplanned, and teen pregnancies account for about one-fifth of all unintended pregnancies each year (Guttmacher Institute, 2012a). Young adults (15–24) only make up about a quarter of the sexually active population, yet they account for nearly half of the sexually transmitted infection (STI) cases annually (Guttmacher Institute, 2012a).

So, teens are having sex. Let's just get that on the table, okay? They're having sex. They're having sex, they're contracting STIs (including very serious ones—in 2008 about 17 percent of the patients receiving an HIV/AIDS diagnosis were young people, age 13–24 [Guttmacher Institute, 2012a]), and they're getting pregnant. And let's be especially clear on this point: *teens are having sex even in states where abstinence-only sex education is the norm.* If you view teenage sex as a problem (and a good many adults do), the "solution" is largely improved teen contraceptive use, not abstinence. While teen birthrates have indeed been on the decline, research in 2007 found that 86 percent of the decline in pregnancy risk between 1995 and 2002 was the result of improved contraceptive use (Santelli et al., 2007).

But let's back up a bit. Where are teens getting their information about sex? If they're sexually active, how do they know about birth control, or the risk of pregnancy and STIs? If they're not yet sexually active, what are they hearing about sex—both positive and negative? Who do they turn to if they're confused, or curious, or anxious about sex? If your answers were the Internet, the Internet, the Internet, and the Internet, you may be surprised.

Teens and Sexual Health Information

You might think that teens growing up in an age with ubiquitous information access coinciding with cuts to sexual education in schools might look online for all their sexual health questions. Yet a recent study suggests that teens—even those with access to high-speed Internet at home, who go online on a daily basis—view sexual health information on the Internet with skepticism, and prefer to rely on school, friends, and family members for answers about sexual health. The research also suggests teens may not actively seek out sexual health information on the web unless they are prompted to do so for a school assignment, despite the increasing number of high-quality websites aimed specifically at teens (Jones and Biddlecom, 2011).

Relying on school for sexual health answers may be dangerous, of course, thanks to a lack of comprehensive sex education programs nationwide. As of 2010, only 20 states and the District of Columbia mandated sex and HIV education. Thirty-seven states require abstinence to be taught in sex education, and no state requires that contraception be stressed (although 18 states and the District of Columbia require contraception to be *included* in sex education) (Guttmacher Institute, 2012b). It may also be difficult to find sexual health information (even for a school assignment!) within the school building, as many schools use filters so aggressive that legitimate websites referring to sex or anatomy are filtered along with pornography and hate speech. We've come a long way since the earliest filters made searching for "breast" (as in "breast cancer") impossible, but the American Civil Liberties Union (ACLU) still has to defend teens' rights to access LGBT websites (ACLU, 2011), and Sex Work Awareness is currently undertaking research to determine the extent to which public library filters block access to information about sexuality and sexual health (Sex Work Awareness, 2011).

Peers and family aren't always the best resources, either. Most of us can remember hearing outlandish descriptions of "sex" from friends or acquaintances when we were young and may not have known better. (Pro tip: Anyone starting a story with "I heard you can't get pregnant if . . . " probably doesn't have your best interests in mind.) Parents who are uncomfortable with the topic may share very little information, if any at all, erring instead on the side of moral imperatives. (Good girls don't get pregnant; boys will do "the right thing.") Although 70 percent of male teens and 79 percent of female teens report talking to a parent about a sexual health issue (Guttmacher Institute, 2012b), a significant number of parents greatly underestimate the effectiveness of contraception in preventing pregnancy and the spread of STIs (Eisenberg et al., 2004). So what's the library's role in sexual health education? Filling in the gaps.

Support Teens' Sexual Health at the Library

One of the easiest ways to position your library as a partner in promoting teen sexual health is to add online health resources to your library's web presence. While we already established that teens might not independently seek out health resources online, if they see your list of recommended websites next to the databases and book lists they already know and trust, your teen patrons will know where to go when they want answers online.

You can also add pamphlets and brochures to your library's other passive displays and handouts. Include local clinic information and hotline numbers, and make sure teens know which services are free and confidential. Teens in some cities can even text clinics for tips, hours, and other information (see, e.g., Internet Sexuality Information Services at http://www.sextextsf.org/). Just be sure to keep all your information current, particularly when it comes to brochures; a bunch of after-school special photos featuring acid-washed jeans are liable to run your teens off laughing, and damage the library's credibility.

It's important to remember that conversations about sex and sexual health are also going to include teens questioning their sexuality and identity. Make sure that your collection includes titles on LGBTQ health and issues. This is another area where currency is key, as older titles may discuss queer identities as abnormal or unhealthy. You may choose to have a separate section for all LGBTQ resources, in the library and online, or you may want to fold in resources where appropriate under health, relationships, or any other category your library uses that may apply. Consider displaying safe space stickers (GLSEN, 2012) or other visible markers that affirm your commitment to the library as a safe place for *all* teens.

So far we've discussed passive approaches—all resources you can offer your teens without really even having to look them in the eye. But what happens when a teen approaches you with a question or a story, and it suddenly dawns on you that you're talking about sex?

- **Listen.** This is probably going to be the first suggestion for every topic, so get used to seeing it in the chapters ahead—but for this topic especially, your first job is to listen. And more than some other issues, this one might make you want to shut your ears. It has nothing to do with being a prude (although you may very well be one when it comes to other people's sex lives)—you might just feel like this isn't any of your business. *Isn't what happens in the privacy of your own home, well, private?* The teen who walks up and launches into a story about making out with her boyfriend and how things got, you know, *serious*, isn't telling you this to brag. (Well, probably not, although if she doesn't have anyone else to tell about her first time, that might be a small part of it.) You need to keep your mouth shut and listen for a minute if you want to identify what this teen needs.
- **Let go of your inner prude.** You have every right to request that a teen not use vulgar language with you, just as you would in any old conversation. But if the topic is sex, there's a very good chance that things are going to get graphic— and if you don't talk about specific parts and who did what with whom, you're

not going to be able to give good advice or point that teen in the direction of the appropriate resources. This is absolutely the right time to ask if the teen would like some more privacy for this conversation, and it might also help to ask if one of his or her friends or another coworker could join. (This strategy can be especially effective if you want to bring in someone who shares that teen's gender, which might make the conversation a little less awkward.) But if you cringe at the mention of body parts or particular sexual acts, you're immediately telling the teen you can't handle this conversation.

- **Stay neutral.** A teen might disclose a risky behavior to you, and your gut reaction might be to yell, "Do you have any idea how *dangerous* that is?" Cool your jets. What's done is done; you can let a teen know about potential risks without shaming him or her for something that's already happened. Anything you say that makes you come across as scolding, disgusted, or judgmental almost guarantees that a teen won't come to you again for advice. And letting your own morals take over the conversation means that you're not paying attention to *this* teen in *these* circumstances. Remember that you're not giving advice to a younger version of you—you're bringing the benefit of experience and a bit of distance to a teen struggling with unique circumstances.

- **Get to the point.** A teen might tell you a story and then sit there staring at you. You're sweating a little, thinking maybe you missed the question, wondering if you're supposed to say something. Sometimes teens blurt out some details and just assume you'll know what they want to ask. (Remember that reference patron with the rash?) Other times teens don't really *have* a question—they want to confide in someone, and they will most likely listen if you have advice or next steps in mind, but mostly they're looking to be reassured. So, be reassuring. Always let teens know you're really glad they talked to you about this. Try a neutral question, such as, "How do you feel about that?" You can be more pointed—"Do you think you need to talk to a doctor?"—but if you're too far out in left field the teen might be frustrated that you're not connecting the dots. As in a reference interview, or in trying to recommend a book for a teen who wants something "good" to read, you might have to ask a few more questions to nudge the conversation along. Just be gentle, and remember that sometimes you're just offering a little prompt so that the teen can tell more of the story.

- **Bring in reinforcements.** Some teens will preface a story with "You can't tell anybody else, but . . . " or try to spring that on you after the story has already been told. It's really important that you let teens know that you respect their privacy, but you can't keep secrets, particularly if you think someone might be hurt. You can try to avoid scaring teens off on that point by asking, "Do you think it'd be okay if we talked to _____ together about this?" Fill in the blank with whoever's appropriate—maybe a coworker they trust, or a teacher, or even a parent. Asking about sharing the conversation, rather than just going ahead and talking to another adult and leaving teens feeling betrayed, lets teens know you care about getting their permission, but this also makes it clear that you think you need some extra help.

- **Keep their trust.** One exception to my confidentiality rule: I think it's absolutely okay to let teens come out to you and not to other adults. If teens ask you to keep their sexuality quiet, there's probably a good reason. You might actually be putting a teen's home life in jeopardy if you tell the wrong person that the teen is queer. Even if you think other people already know (and plenty of adults, particularly queer adults, think they "know" when a teen is gay), wait for a teen's permission or until he or she makes it clear it's okay to share. Outing a teen, even by accident, can be extremely dangerous and may alienate you from that teen (and others) for a long time.

- **Find answers together.** You may find that a teen asks you something that has you completely stumped. While it's tempting to pretend that you have all the answers, it's a better idea to admit that you're at a loss—but that you have some good ideas of where to start. Showing a teen that you still have a strategy even when you don't know where to turn helps model searching skills. And sometimes watching an adult using a book or website, even if it was sitting right there under "Health and Sexuality" this whole time, lends that resource sudden credibility. By searching for answers together, you're also likely to get more information from the teen than if you just sent the teen to a computer or handed him or her the number of a clinic. Maybe the first few snippets the teen told you weren't the *whole* story, or maybe looking at a website together will make the teen remember a detail that didn't seem important before. Either way, you're showing your teens that you're invested in finding them the right answer, not just in getting them to leave your desk.

- **Crack the code.** Any young adult librarian can tell you about the hilarious litany of ways teens can ask about sex without actually *asking about sex*. Sometimes they're just looking for a book—you know, one about, um, relationships? But not like, *relationships*, I mean, not like *drama*, but, you know…girls who are with guys? You know, like *with* guys? (Seriously, this is one that can go around in circles for *hours* if you let it. You will become a master of translating *meaningful emphasis*.) The same can be true when teens have questions about sex or their bodies. Again, be gentle—there's a good chance there's some heavy-duty embarrassment and even shame coloring this conversation—but also give teens some options for answering their questions without talking to a librarian. Leave certain books available for browsing, maybe in a somewhat private area of the library. (I recommend leaving *Body Drama* [Redd, 2008] and *Sex: A Book for Teens* [Hasler, 2010] highly visible, although sometimes that can get a wee bit awkward if the senior center uses your space for evening activities. Not that this has ever happened to me in real life or anything. Nope. Not at all.)

- **Respect your teens.** Whether it's respecting their chosen pronouns or supporting a pregnancy decision you disagree with, you have to show your teens that you can help them no matter what. Part of that means proving that you won't tolerate disrespect from others. Some of the most difficult confrontations you have with teens can be your interventions when you hear them disrespecting others. Whether they're calling things gay or retarded or swearing creatively enough to make a sailor blush, teens can say some really hurtful things. And on a daily basis, you'll have a decision to make: do I pretend I didn't hear that, or do I do something about it?

You will discover exactly what a teen (or an adult) has to say to make you lose your cool. Maybe it's a racial epithet you thought was long dead. Maybe it's a jab at a less fortunate teen. Maybe it hits below the belt at your own identity. Whatever it is, I can guarantee you that at some point you will find yourself yelling across the library for someone to cut it out. And there's something to be said for that. Yes, you run the risk of more manipulative teens knowing exactly how to push your buttons. You also run the risk of feeling guilty or ridiculous for the rest of the day, unable to put your finger on exactly what made you so mad. But if you blow your stack once at the word *fag*, there's also a good chance that a gay teen in the library feels some sense of relief, that for once this word did not go unnoticed and unpunished.

A more middle-of-the-road approach is to make one of your YA area expectations that the space will be free of disrespectful language. This gives you more or less carte blanche to call out any language that could be construed as disrespecting *someone*. It can be helpful to set up your rules (and your own interventions when the rules are broken) this way because it frames the infraction as one against *everyone*, not just against *you*. If teens know you as that librarian who yells if someone says something's gay, yes, they might not use homophobic language in the library, but only because they don't want you to yell at them. They're not really given any context to see the behavior *itself* as wrong, only the behavior *in this time and place* as a problem.

A strategy for combating offensive language, whether it's homophobic, sexist, racist, or some other color of hateful, is to actually have a conversation about it. Many teens don't really know the literal meaning of the words they throw around so casually. I once tried to engage a young man who'd referred to someone as "acting like a fag," and he quickly pointed out that he hadn't called anything *gay*, so what was the big deal? You don't owe anyone who uses hate speech your patience and calm civility, but when you can engage teens in a nonconfrontational manner, asking them to really think about the words they use and the impact they might have on those around them, you may be surprised by their capacity for empathy and deep thought.

Still feeling ill-equipped to tackle a conversation about pregnancy, coming out to parents, or what constitutes third base? Here are some resources to bring you up to speed, and share with teens in your library.

Go-To Sources for Research and Current Data on Sex and Sexuality (Adult Level)

- **Guttmacher Institute** (http://www.guttmacher.org/)
  You can find great data, including quick fact sheets, on a variety of topics relating to sexual and reproductive health.
- **Mayo Clinic** (http://www.mayoclinic.com/)
  Online resources from one of the leading medical authorities. Includes facts and figures on individual diseases and conditions, as well as potential symptoms.

Health Databases Geared Toward Teens

- **Rosen's Teen Health & Wellness** (http://www.teenhealthandwellness.com/)
  Each topic comes with a variety of different articles, all reviewed by professionals. Articles may be a little lighter on hard data in their effort to be digestible to teens, but they do provide a good overview of the issues.
- **Gale Health & Wellness Resource Center** (http://www.gale.cengage.com/Health/HealthRC/about.htm)
  This database offers a variety of ways into a subject, from diseases and conditions to individual health assessments and links to other trusted medical sites. Some of the articles and overviews can come off as a bit clinical or technical, but all the facts are there.

Sex and Sexuality Websites Geared Toward Teens

- **Scarleteen** (http://www.scarleteen.com/)
  Scarleteen (tagline: "Sex ed for the real world") is a great website with a lot to offer teens. Teens can share their stories, get frank answers to questions all about sex and reproductive health, take quizzes and polls to gauge their sexual knowledge, and even find a doctor—all in a space geared toward and safe for young adults.
- **Sex, Etc.** (http://www.sexetc.org/)
  Sex, Etc. is a magazine and website by teens, for teens. It features frequently asked questions (FAQs) on a variety of topics, a guide to state-by-state information on sex ed and teen rights, info on how to get tested for STIs, and much more.
- **Planned Parenthood** (http://www.plannedparenthood.org/)
  While the Planned Parenthood site has a lot to offer readers of any age, the section for teens offers very straightforward information on topics geared toward teens, from information about pregnancy or relationships to an easy forum to ask experts any question. The website also makes it extremely easy to find a nearby Planned Parenthood health center.

- **Midwest Teen Sex Show** (http://midwestteensexshow.com/)
  Nikol Hasler and company produced 25 episodes of what is basically the most hilarious (yet informative) sex ed class of all time. It's not intended to be stand-alone sex ed—they prefer to think of it as "sex information," not sex education—but it does a great job of introducing controversial (and potentially embarrassing, thus left out of sex conversations) topics and making them approachable for teens and adults alike.
- **Go Ask Alice!** (http://www.goaskalice.columbia.edu/)
  A product of the Health Services at Columbia University, Go Ask Alice! offers visitors answers to a huge variety of questions—and the opportunity to ask their own. The style is conversational but informative, and answers are extremely thorough. Answers aren't geared strictly toward teens, but the style easily fits those new to sex or considering sexual activity.

Books You Should Have in Your Collection

- Hasler, Nikol. 2010. *Sex: A Book for Teens: An Uncensored Guide to Your Body, Sex, and Safety*. San Francisco: Zest Books.
  From the creator of Midwest Teen Sex Show comes a very, *very* straightforward book for teens covering just about every topic on sex and sexuality under the sun. Teens might pick it up for the cows humping on the cover, but they'll check it out (or slip it out secretly) to read all about the terms they've heard but just assumed everyone else understood.
- Redd, Nancy Amanda. 2008. *Body Drama*. New York: Gotham.
  Redd teamed up with a physician specializing in adolescent health issues to give girls a book all about their bodies and the questions they may be too embarrassed to ask a parent or doctor. With full color photos and diagrams and solutions to common health and image problems, it's only a shame that Redd hasn't yet offered boys a helpful handbook of their own.

With all the resources listed here, or any others you already use in your library, it's always a good idea to give yourself some time to approach a question the way a teen would. As adults, we often take for granted our autopilot skills when it comes to seeking out information. We have trusted sources for all kinds of topics, whether it's using IMDB to figure out what other movies that actor has been in or using online reminders to keep track of our periods. Even if we don't know where to begin we know where *not* to begin, knowing that certain search engines are more likely to produce news and shopping results or deciding we're not looking for the kind of academic difficulty a particular database is likely to offer. Teens, on the other hand, may not have developed these same skills yet.

Sit down sometime with a sample question. *Can you get pregnant if you use a condom?* Think about how a teen might try to find the answer to that question. Would he type it in, word-for-word, into a search engine? Would she look for a related article on *Wikipedia*? If he navigated to one of the health and sexuality resources from the library site, would he see anything on the webpage that resembled an answer to the question? At some point, would she get frustrated and just give up?

The whole point in youth services, of course, is to ensure that no teen ever gives up—and that the young adult librarian never gives up on teens. In order for that to be true when teens have questions or concerns about sex and sexuality, you may have to adjust your comfort zone. You have to remember to listen, offer information where it's needed, and reserve judgment. You don't have to be alone in supporting teens' sexual health, just as *they* don't have to be alone when they need help the most. You may need to lighten the mood with some pictures of humping cows, but hey, that's the joy of working with teens.

References

ACLU (American Civil Liberties Union). 2011. "Don't Filter Me: Web Content Filtering in Schools." ACLU. Accessed July 7. http://www.aclu.org/dont-filter-me-web-content-filtering-schools.

Centers for Disease Control and Prevention. 2011. "Teen Birth Rates Declined Again in 2009." Centers for Disease Control and Prevention. Last updated July 1. http://www.cdc.gov/features/dsTeenPregnancy/.

Eisenberg. Marla E., Linda H. Bearinger, Renee E. Sieving, Carolyne Swain, and Michael D. Resnick. 2004. "Parents' Beliefs about Condoms and Oral Contraceptives: Are They Medically Accurate?" *Perspectives on Sexual and Reproductive Health* 36, no. 2. Guttmacher Institute. http://www.guttmacher.org/pubs/journals/3605004.html.

GLSEN (Gay, Lesbian and Straight Education Network). 2012. "Safe Space Kit." Accessed July 7, 2011. http://www.glsen.org/cgi-bin/iowa/all/news/record/1641.html.

Guttmacher Institute. 2012a. "Facts on American Teens' Sexual and Reproductive Health." Guttmacher Institute. February. http://www.guttmacher.org/pubs/FB-ATSRH.html.

———. 2012b. "Facts on American Teens' Sources of Information about Sex." Guttmacher Institute. February. http://www.guttmacher.org/pubs/FB-Teen-Sex-Ed.html.

Hasler, Nikol. 2010. *Sex: A Book for Teens: An Uncensored Guide to Your Body, Sex, and Safety*. San Francisco: Zest Books.

Jones, Rachel K., and Biddlecom, Ann E. 2011. "Is the Internet Filling the Sexual Health Information Gap for Teens? An Exploratory Study." *Journal of Health Communication: International Perspectives* 16, no. 2. http://www.tandfonline.com/doi/abs/10.1080/10810730.2010.535112.

Redd, Nancy Amanda. 2008. *Body Drama*. New York: Gotham.

Santelli, John S., Laura Duberstein Lindberg, Lawrence B. Finer, and Susheela Singh. 2007. "Explaining Recent Declines in Adolescent Pregnancy in the United States: The Contribution of Abstinence and Improved Contraceptive Use." *The American Journal of Public Health* 97, no. 1. http://www.ncbi.nlm.nih.gov/pmc/articles/PMC1716232/.

Sex Work Awareness. 2011. "Sex and the Library: A Research Study on Sexuality Information Access in U.S. Public Libraries." Sexuality Information Access in U.S. Public Libraries. Accessed July 7. http://www.infoandthelibrary.org/.

4

"Does That Girl Even Have a House?"—Homeless Teens

The Numbers

The United States Code defines "homeless" or "homeless person" or "homeless individual" as any individual who lacks a fixed, regular, and adequate nighttime residence, as well as anyone whose primary nighttime residence is a shelter, an institution housing individuals who are to be institutionalized, or any public or private place not intended to be a regular sleeping accommodation for human beings (HUD, 2011). Under this definition, national estimates of adult homelessness vary greatly. In 2009, *USA Today* estimated that 1.6 million people used transitional housing or emergency shelters (National Coalition for the Homeless, 2009). Two years earlier, the National Law Center on Homelessness and Poverty approximated that 3.5 million people were likely to experience homelessness in a given year (National Coalition for the Homeless, 2009). These numbers might not seem so large in comparison to the total U.S. population—even the larger of the two estimates only translates to about 1 percent of the United States—but we're still talking about *millions* of Americans without regular, adequate shelter. And many of those Americans are children or teens.

The most recent study released by the Office of Juvenile Justice and Delinquency Prevention in the U.S. Department of Justice reported an estimated 1,682,900 homeless and runaway youth (National Coalition for the Homeless, 2008). In a 2010 Covenant House Institute report on homeless youth, 38 percent of homeless youth report past physical abuse, while 26 percent (40 percent of females) report sexual abuse. Forty-one percent have a history of foster or institutional placement, with an average of six years in the system; 28 percent report past psychiatric hospitalization; 36 percent have a family history of mental health issues; 56 percent have a family history of substance abuse; and 51 percent have been arrested (Covenant House Institute, 2010). Somewhere between 6 and 22 percent of homeless youth are pregnant. Estimates for HIV infection among homeless youth are usually around 5 percent, but one study of homeless youth in San Francisco found 17 percent infected (National

Coalition for the Homeless, 2008). These numbers should rattle you, but it only gets worse when we look at homeless youth who identify as lesbian, gay, bisexual, or transgender (LGBT, or queer).

According to the Center for American Progress, while LGBT teens make up roughly 5 to 7 percent of the overall youth population, LGBT youth make up between 7 and 39 percent of total homeless youth. Sixty-two percent of queer homeless youth attempt suicide, compared with 29 percent of their heterosexual homeless peers. Homeless LGBT youth suffer higher rates of alcohol abuse, injectable drug use, unprotected sex, and HIV infection. One study even suggests that gay homeless youth are more likely to suffer from depression, while lesbian homeless youth are more likely to suffer from post-traumatic stress disorder (PTSD) (Quintana, Rosenthal, and Krehely, 2010). Even more staggering: while the Covenant House puts the average homeless youth at ages 18–19 (Covenant House Institute, 2010), the average gay youth first becomes homeless at age 14. The average transgender youth becomes homeless at just 13 (Quintana, Rosenthal, and Krehely, 2010). Blacks in particular are overrepresented even in the overall homeless youth population, but particularly among homeless LGBT youth; gay youth are approximately 44 percent black and 26 percent Hispanic, while transgender youth are 62 percent black and 20 percent Hispanic (Quintana, Rosenthal, and Krehely, 2010).

So where do these heartbreaking statistics leave those of us who work with teens? No doubt the numbers make you want to reach out to the homeless teens in your community, but while many of us may think we can quickly spot homeless adults on the sidewalk (or in the reference room), runaway and homeless teens may not be nearly so easy to see—and for some very good reasons.

- **It's temporary.** Homeless teens may try to keep their living situation a secret because, like many homeless adults, they believe it's temporary; things will get better tomorrow, or in a few days, or next week. And they might be right—part of the difficulty in obtaining accurate estimates for the number of homeless at any given time is how quickly, and how often, homeless individuals' living situations may change. The numbers of those in shelters and other emergency housing will inevitably rise in colder months in many cities, where the very same shelter patrons may sleep outdoors in warmer months. Teens who are homeless because their parents can't find stable housing may have no bed one night but a place to stay the next. Of course, even if the situation *is* temporary, teens—like adults—who are homeless once are more likely to become homeless again.
- **It's better than nothing.** Homeless teens, particularly those who might be defined as runaways (leaving the home or living situation independently, rather than becoming homeless with adults as part of a family), may be struggling, but those struggles may seem better than whatever prompted them to leave home in the first place. Remember those statistics about homeless youth and family history

of mental illness or alcohol abuse? Even worse are the numbers of teens who flee home (or foster home) after physical or sexual abuse. The National Coalition for the Homeless finds that unstable family conditions are the number-one reason that teens leave home. In one U.S. Department of Health and Human Services study, more than half of the youth interviewed during a shelter stay reported that their parents either told them to leave or knew they were leaving and didn't try to stop them (National Coalition for the Homeless, 2008).

- **They have a record.** Remember that more than half of all homeless youth have been arrested at some point. In many cases, they may have been picked up by the police while homeless—for sleeping in public, for breaking youth curfews, or for engaging in criminal activity. This means that even if a given teen hasn't been in trouble with the police, they likely know someone who has. They may be less likely to disclose to you because they fear that your first step will be calling the police, and they'll be taken (possibly taken back, for the second or multiple time) to a juvenile detention facility, where they may face physical and sexual abuse. If they're currently on parole or probation—as approximately 9 percent of homeless youth are—they may be even more frightened of law enforcement (and, thus, wary of disclosing their living situation to an adult).

- **They're making it work.** There are also some homeless teens who try to stay in hiding not merely because they don't want to go "home" (wherever that may be), but also because they believe they've found a better life on the street. Particularly in larger urban areas, youth street culture may embrace homeless or runaway teens, offering them a sense of family and protection that they never had with biological (or state-mandated) family. It's foolish (and dangerous) to believe that all or even most homeless people, whether adult or youth, *want* to be homeless, but it's shortsighted to believe that none of them do. Many of the other factors listed above may still be at play—abusive parents, a sexuality or gender identity that isn't accepted, problems with crime or mental illness—but the teen may also feel that the new life they're leading is much better than the alternatives.

- **They need help.** Homeless teens may also hide their homelessness because they're struggling with mental illness, alcohol or drug addiction, or because they're trying to cover for a sibling or friend who is *also* homeless. Any of these issues can impair a teen's judgment, increase paranoia, and lead them to fear adult involvement with them or their friends and family.

For any or all of these reasons, homeless and runaway teens can act as chameleons, blending in with their peers so that no adult—no matter how well-intentioned—can uncover their secret and involve the police or other authorities. So what are some of the signs to look for that might suggest a teen is homeless?

- **They're always "staying with friends."** Although they might not be included in official estimates of homelessness, teens who spend their time moving from one couch or floor to the next certainly don't have a stable living situation. They may even be staying with other teen peers without their friends' parents or family knowing anything about the sleepovers, meaning they still don't have a safe place to store belongings or take a shower. This solution might seem like a step above staying in a shelter, where most homeless people must keep a close eye on their belongings and report back promptly to claim a bed, but teens who move from friend to friend nonetheless aren't improving their chances of finding a stable living situation. Be on the lookout for teens who are hesitant to provide an address or who seem to always be talking about a different friend with whom they're staying. Teens who are desperate may even end up staying with friends of friends—adult acquaintances they've barely met, or true strangers—which can leave them more vulnerable to sexual abuse or exploitation.

- **They're at the library, not at school.** Homeless teens, particularly those who become homeless with other members of their family, may float from school to school as their tenuous living situations change. They may have difficulty enrolling due to lack of a fixed address, and their credits may not transfer from school to school, leaving them far behind their peer group whenever they're able to attend classes. As a result, many homeless teens drop out altogether. But if they're living in an emergency shelter, or staying with a friend whose parents don't know about the arrangement, they probably have nowhere to go during the day. Public librarians who work with teens are used to spotting truants, but a teen skipping class may not simply be out of school for the day. Look for teens who hesitate to name their school (or can't come up with one at all), or change their story frequently when they're spotted in the library.

- **They make no mention of family.** Particularly with teens you've come to know better, who may even confide in you on certain topics, it should stand out when a teen *never* mentions family or home life. Teens who became homeless with their family may be ashamed of their parents or their situation, while teens who ran away from abusive or exploitative families or guardians might simply not want to be reminded of them. Either way, a teen who is purposefully leaving their family or home life out of the conversation may be terrified that you'd try to contact relatives if you knew who—or *where*—they were.

- **They have poor personal hygiene.** As I mentioned earlier, teens who are staying with friends may be in hiding from adults and can't safely use the shower or shave. Teens staying in emergency shelters may balk at long lines to bathe—many shelters tightly regulate times when clients can use the showers—or fear having their possessions taken from them while they're in the shower. And, of course, teens who sleep outdoors may have no access to bathroom facilities at all. While homeless teens, like homeless adults, may resort to stop-gap measures such as bathing in public bathrooms or trying to wash clothes in a sink, they may not be entirely successful. Look for teens who don't seem to be washing their hair or shaving regularly. Also be on the lookout for teens who seem to frequently repeat the same clothes or outfits, as it may mean they only have a limited set of clothes and no access to adequate laundry services.

- **They're always there at closing time.** Especially for teens staying at emergency shelters with late check-in times, homeless teens may be looking for free places to kill much of their daytime hours. Particularly in public libraries with hours that extend into the evening, you should pay attention to teens who seem determined to stay in the building—and not because they're working on a big project or paper for school. These teens may also fall asleep in the library, especially if they've been too tense to sleep well in a shelter or other temporary bed.

- **They carry it all.** No doubt you're used to seeing teens with big backpacks. Textbooks, notebooks, art supplies, athletic gear, musical instruments—a busy teen is a teen with a lot of baggage. But what if those aren't school supplies in those bags? Teens with no stable housing have to bring all of their things with them or risk losing them. Teens who are carrying excessive clothing or personal keepsakes—or who seem to perpetually be carrying an overnight bag—may not just be going on a sleepover.

Helping Homeless Teens

If you spot any of these potential signs of homelessness, what's your next step? First, try to engage this teen in conversation before you get other adults (and authorities) involved. Any of these signs taken independently, or even in combination, could be symptoms of an entirely different issue—for example, poor personal grooming can also be a sign of depression. Talking with the teen will give you a better idea of whether your hunch was correct. Talking—and *listening*—can also show teens that you care about them and have their best interests in mind, which will help greatly if you need to get in touch with the police or social services. Getting in touch with these agencies *together*, rather than reporting on teens on your own, shows teens that you believe they should be involved in the decisions that affect them.

As for the reporting itself, that could take many forms. Whether you work in a public library, school library, or another setting altogether, your workplace should have a policy on mandatory reporting. Those of us who work in schools might have initially been nervous about the idea of reporting: How do we know that a young person is in danger, or might be a danger toward someone else? Whom do we call? Are we supposed to just tell the police and hope for the best? While it's important to know the exact language in your workplace's policy (most use the standard that you must report if you believe a child has been hurt or will be hurt), you can also relax a little.

Mandatory reporting doesn't mean that you're going to have a direct line to the police commissioner. It means that when you suspect that one of the teens you work with has been hurt or is in danger, the story shouldn't end with you. It's your responsibility to make sure that *someone* else in the building knows what you know, whether that's a school nurse, a supervisor, a guidance counselor, or a police officer. Telling another adult, especially one who already knows the teen in question, can help confirm or clear up your suspicions. And by seeking out someone with more expertise in the proper field—whether that's social work, mental health, or law enforcement—you can lessen the burden on yourself. You might think that your bond with a teen means you need to be everything you can, but remember that there are other trained professionals who help teens for a living.

That said, it's important to know just who the local authorities are when it comes to outreach and social services for teens. Find the neighborhood police station closest to your library, and see if they have an officer or a unit dedicated to working with youth. Find out what *they* have to say about your community's population of homeless and runaway teens. The police are likely used to seeing these teens out and about, but you see a different side of these teens when they're in your library. Ask the police what they think about reporting truants or homeless youth. By asking these questions before you have a particular teen or group of teens in mind, you can speak to police officers when they're neutral on the subject, rather than right after a confrontation when they may have strong feelings about particular teens.

Find the nearest Department of Children and Families (DCF), however that agency is defined in your community. Ask them about the most common issues where they work. Do they have to do a lot of repeat foster placements? How often do they deal with runaways? Do they see more teens experiencing homelessness along with family members, or teens living on the street independently? Again, asking these questions without a particular teen in mind gives you a better idea of what to expect should you have to contact DCF or social services in an emergency. Getting comfortable with these agencies can also help you discuss potential options with a teen in crisis. A homeless teen who has been in an unbearable group home may not know that there are other foster options, or may not understand his legal rights once he turns 18 after having been in foster placement or a ward of the state.

Get to know your local homeless shelters and drop-in centers. Many organizations that focus on issues other than homelessness, such as suicide prevention or mental health, may also have a limited number of beds or other services for homeless youth. Find out if your homeless shelters reserve beds for teens and children. I've talked a lot in this chapter about homeless teens accessing emergency shelters, but the truth of the matter is that very few shelters in this country can accommodate unaccompanied minors. Even if they do, they may have a waiting list months long. Although children and teens who become homeless with their parents or relatives have options in shelters and housing assistance, teens—particularly those under 16 and those who have been labeled runaways—have far fewer options. Find out if any of the adult drop-in centers in your community accept teens, and find out if any of them have laundry or shower facilities. Even if a particular group can't offer homeless teens a bed, they may at least be able to offer them a shower, a washer and dryer, or a hot meal.

Whether your community has the best social services in the country or barely anything to offer those less fortunate, there's a good chance you will serve homeless teens—and adults—in your library. Aside from connecting homeless teens to community partners who may be able to help them, you also need to make sure that your library is a safe space for everyone, and that homeless patrons and other patrons can peacefully coexist.

- **Keep valuables safe.** Many libraries and archives that restrict what patrons can bring into certain areas—no pens in the reading room, for example, or no food—offer secure locker space, and it's not a bad idea for all libraries. Offering patrons a locked place to store belongings can reduce the risk of theft and make sure that certain items (smelly foods or dirty laundry) aren't brought into common spaces. Some locker rentals charge only a deposit, returned when the key is returned, but you may also want to offer teens free or reduced rates.
- **Maintain passive resources.** It's great to have brochures out on a desk or up on a bulletin board, but for issues such as homelessness it's also important to give teens information in more private areas. Put hotline numbers and shelter information in restrooms, and make sure your custodial staff checks these frequently to make sure they haven't been removed or defaced. You can expand on this information on your library website.
- **Encourage interaction.** It's important for your staff—including security personnel—to interact with teens in a variety of ways, not just during a crisis situation. Do you leave your desk often? Do you offer help to patrons only when they approach you, or do you make yourself available in other ways? Do you talk to your security staff so that they know your policies and mission, or do you only call them in when there's a problem? Teens who see adults in the library as real people, with emotions and concerns, are less likely to see them as authority figures who only want to maintain order.
- **Maintain privacy.** Your workplace's policies may mandate that you talk to other adults when a teen is in crisis, but that doesn't mean you need to gossip—or that you need to tell other *teens* about anyone's issues. Be discreet. Just as your patrons' circulation records are private, their lives should be, too. It's natural for teens (and adults) to want to know what's happening if they see police arrive or if an emergency happens in the library, but it's not your place to share details about a teen's home situation unnecessarily.
- **Keep a free stash.** Many libraries and other public institutions already stock free items such as extra pens and pencils for patrons, and their public bathrooms

may hold tissues, women's hygiene products, and even free condoms. Why not hit the travel aisle of your local drugstore and grab cheap deodorant, travel toothpaste and brushes, and shaving cream? Critics might worry that having these available in a public restroom will only encourage homeless individuals to bathe there, but it's also likely that the people who need them will just take them discreetly and leave.

It's important to note that many people—patrons as well as librarians—have strong reactions to homeless individuals using the library. They may react to personal odor, complain if homeless people seem to monopolize computers or other resources, or even accuse homeless individuals of theft or mental illness. While the data cited earlier suggests that homeless youth may indeed suffer higher levels of alcohol and drug abuse, mental illness, and arrest or incarceration, that doesn't mean all homeless teens are violent or dangerous—or that they don't have every right to your library's resources.

Here's where some librarians get very uncomfortable. I've heard school librarians in particular lament the loss of books and other library resources (this is actually often framed in terms of *theft*, not *loss*) when homeless or itinerant students check out items and never return to school, likely because their family housing situation has changed drastically. For younger children especially, calling this *theft* isn't entirely fair; children are almost completely dependent upon their parents or guardians, and once a family moves out of one neighborhood (whether to a shelter or to another temporary home), most children would have no way of traveling the distance alone to return library items. (Parents experiencing homelessness, for their part, likely have more pressing concerns than a lost library book; they are likely to be unemployed and may not have access to reliable transportation.)

For homeless and runaway teens, perhaps we might assume a greater responsibility to return items, but again, these teens have a lot on their minds. When you're not sure where your next shower or meal might come from and you're closely guarding your *own* possessions, renewing a library book might seem much less pressing. Yet perhaps it's not so important *that* homeless teens—or any teens, really, as all kinds of teens can walk off with a book or DVD and never come back—may lose or steal items, but *which* items they take.

I do want to acknowledge that the loss of items, whether you want to frame it as loss or theft, is frustrating and costly. Building a collection only to have parts of it disappear, especially when patrons are unlikely to replace or pay for the items, can be extremely disheartening. But ask yourself this: What are patrons taking? Is there a pattern? Are you having a hard time keeping books on certain topics on the shelves? Some librarians identify certain issues or authors as "high-theft" material, and begin to treat them differently from the rest of the collection, keeping them in sight of the reference desk or even restricting them to an office or storeroom, forcing teens who want these items to come up and ask for them specifically. While this strategy may reduce loss, it will likely also discourage many teens from ever accessing material they may desperately need, such as material on sex and sexuality. Indeed, shame and embarrassment about these topics lead many teens to "steal" such books rather than have an adult know they want to read them.

Above all, remember that if your patrons are taking items and never returning them, *you are doing something right*. You're providing materials that your patrons want and need. Yes, you may need to replace them frequently, and it would be great if the teens you serve felt comfortable enough to tell you when they want information about STIs or drug abuse, but take comfort in the fact that at least these items are reaching the very teens who may need them the most.

Resources for homeless youth vary widely from state to state and even region to region. While some states now have shelters dedicated to homeless LGBT youth, others still don't have enough beds to accommodate any unaccompanied minors. To learn more about homelessness and teen homelessness in the United States, here are two highly recommended resources.

The National Coalition for the Homeless

The National Coalition for the Homeless (http://www.nationalhomeless.org/) is a policy advocacy group dedicated to preventing and ending homelessness as well as protecting the rights of those experiencing homelessness. The National Coalition for the Homeless offers fact sheets, directories of local and national homeless service providers, and information on their ongoing projects.

Covenant House Institute

Founded almost 40 years ago, Covenant House Institute (http://www.covenanthouse .org/) is dedicated to serving homeless teens. With locations across the United States, Covenant House currently serves over 55,000 homeless youth each year, as well as offering research and statistics on youth homelessness. The institute also offers the Nine Line, a hotline for runaway and homeless youth: 1-800-999-9999 (Note: this is a religiously affiliated organization.)

References

Covenant House Institute. 2010. "A National Picture of Youth Homelessness." Covenant House. http://www.covenanthouse.org/sites/default/files/National%20Picture%20of%20Youth %20Homelessness%2010.14.10.pdf.

HUD (U.S. Department of Housing and Urban Development). 2011. "Homeless Emergency Assistance and Rapid Transition to Housing: Defining Homeless, Final Rule." *Federal Register* 76 (December 5): 75995-75997. http://www.hudhre.info/documents/HEARTH_ HomelessDefinition_FinalRule.pdf.

National Coalition for the Homeless. 2008. "Homeless Youth." National Coalition for the Homeless. June. http://www.nationalhomeless.org/factsheets/youth.html.

————. 2009. "How Many People Experience Homelessness?" National Coalition for the Homeless. July. http://www.nationalhomeless.org/factsheets/How_Many.html.

Quintana, Nico Sifra, Josh Rosenthal, and Jeff Krehely. 2010. "On the Streets: The Federal Response to Gay and Transgender Homeless Youth." Center for American Progress. June. http://www.americanprogress.org/issues/2010/06/pdf/lgbtyouthhomelessness.pdf.

5

"Did That Hurt?"— Tattoos and Piercings

Teens and Body Modification

If you have visible tattoos or piercings anywhere other than your ears, you can count on teens asking about them. You'll probably find yourself having the same conversation over and over again, usually prompted by one question: "Did that hurt?" It might seem like a silly question to you—of course getting repeatedly stabbed by needles hurts—but the teen who asks you really wants to know. They may be contemplating a piercing or a tattoo (or they may already have several), or they may just be genuinely curious; some teens who seem the most interested in talking tattoo design or the pros and cons of an eyebrow ring would never actually get one themselves. So how do you talk about body modification without risking the wrath of parents who might not be so thrilled when their son or daughter comes home with a six-inch Spongebob?

First, relax. You'd dispute an adult saying that sex or violence in books gives teens ideas, right? Controversial topics—suicide, abortion, premarital sex—all exist in the real world, not to mention the multimedia world now so integral to most teens' lives. The same holds true for conversations. Examples of tattoos and piercings—for better or worse—are everywhere: celebrities sport them, professional athletes cover themselves in them, and reality shows document the lives of tattoo artists in minute detail. It's far better that a teen hears about the realities of body modification from an adult who cares about their well-being (that *does* describe you, right?) than that he or she only sees the finished product without knowing any of the risks or the care and thought involved. Even if you don't have any tattoos or piercings yourself—and even if you personally think they're a really bad idea—you can still counsel your teens effectively when they want to talk about body modification.

So let's talk about risks. The Food and Drug Administration lists infection, allergic reaction, and MRI complications as potential risks associated with tattooing (U.S. Food and Drug Administration, 2011). Infection is also a concern with body piercing, along with allergies to metals and increased risks for those with preexisting health conditions (Mayo Clinic Staff, 2010a). These risks—and laws regulating tattoo and piercing facilities—mean reputable artists and piercers will thoroughly sterilize equipment and follow basic hygiene procedures (wearing gloves, sterilizing surfaces, and keeping food and drinks away from workstations).

It's also important for teens to know that these risks vary from person to person, so it's a good idea for them to know their own bodies well before introducing a tattoo or piercing into the mix. Do they have any skin conditions that might slow the healing process or make body modification particularly painful? What about problems with scarring? Some people's skin can react to tattooing with raised scars that may never go down to match the surrounding area. Those at risk of blood clots or who are on medication to thin the blood should seek medical advice (as well as the advice of a reputable artist) before attempting any kind of body modification. What about allergies? Most parlors start off with stainless steel for all piercings, because it's considered the most sterile metal, but many teens will want to change to gold or silver once a piercing is healed, and metal allergies should certainly be a concern. Anyone with allergies to dyes (such as the artificial colorings often found in food) should also be cautious when looking for a tattoo, as some of these same pigments may also be present in tattoo ink.

One element that's a little harder to pin down is an individual's tolerance for pain. Many of us—from small children all the way to the toughest adults—have a fear of needles, which are intimately involved in both piercing and tattooing. Yet many of us still choose to get tattoos and piercings. The pain of either depends greatly on the body part involved, how long the piercer or tattoo artist spends working on the piece, and the subject's own pain tolerance. Most piercings take very little time for the actual piercing, and the pain involved seems to vary greatly from person to person (some swear cartilage is much more painful than softer areas like the earlobes, and some assert the exact opposite). Healing, however, may be painful, particularly if the piercing is in an area where it may move around or where its owner may sleep on it. For tattoos, generally speaking, areas where the skin is thinner or where the skin is closer to bone (spots such as the ribs, fingers, toes, chest, and skull, as opposed to fleshier spots such as the arms, legs, or buttocks) are usually more painful than areas where flesh and muscle are thicker.

More sensitive areas (stomachs, anywhere near or on the genitals, ticklish spots such as the underarms) can also be more painful to tattoo. On any body part, however, one person may find the pain excruciating, while another may have no problem grinning and bearing it. The sensation of piercing a body part is unique, but may feel similar to getting a shot or even getting stitches. Tattoos, while applied with needles, don't feel all that similar to medical needles; I've described the sensation as having someone draw on my skin with the pointy end of a (math) compass while having a bad sunburn. In my experience smaller tattoos (particularly those in only one color) are hardly painful at all, while larger tattoos hurt more the longer the session lasts, especially when an artist has to repeatedly go over an area that has already been tattooed. This is common in tattoos with complex color schemes, although tattoos requiring large blocks of single colors also require a considerable amount of work (and, thus, pain). Tattoo artists actually use different types of needles for fine lines and for shading, and the sensation for each is unique. Think of the difference between a very fine paintbrush and one used to apply broad swaths of color. (Only, you know, make the paintbrushes really pointy.) The pain of healing is quite different from the pain of the initial tattoo or piercing. Both can ache or throb for days or even weeks and will most likely be quite sensitive to the touch.

It is, of course, very important not to move when a piercer or tattoo artist is working; what seems like a minor twitch can have a huge impact on the placement of a piercing or the overall design of a tattoo. Most artists understand that their customers, especially first timers, may be nervous, and will do their best to keep everyone calm. Some will talk through the whole process, while others (particularly some tattoo artists) prefer not to be distracted at all while working. Teens may also find that some parlors play music all day, which may or may not be soothing; I've personally been tattooed by artists who listened to everything from Bob Dylan to heavy metal. While it hasn't always been *my* cup of tea, I assume that artists choose the soundtrack that helps *them* focus and stay calm, and that they'll come up with their best work under those conditions.

Reputable parlors employ piercers and artists who take the time to talk with potential customers, even when that customer doesn't plan on getting work done anytime soon. Anyone should be able to walk in off the street and ask about that parlor's safety procedures, what to expect in terms of healing time and discomfort during the piercing or tattoo, and how a new tattoo or piercing may interfere with everyday activities while it heals. It's true that many piercers and tattoo artists closely schedule their appointments, so they may have little time for a lengthy conversation with a walk-in, but teens *should* be able to schedule an appointment (even if it's only for ten minutes or half an hour) to get all their questions answered. Most parlors also employ at least one front-of-house staff member, who often checks in appointments, handles payment, and answers phones; this employee should be willing to answer questions, or point teens toward the artist or piercer with the most expertise in that area. Even if a shop is slammed, reputable artists and employees should be willing to take the time to answer questions or walk teens through any procedure. Anyone in the industry who acts too busy to talk might also be too busy to provide adequate aftercare instructions and shouldn't be trusted for a body- (and potentially life-) altering procedure.

It's worth noting that some tattoo parlors do specialize in custom pieces, usually for customers who already have several tattoos and know the ropes. These parlors are unlikely to offer flash work (work picked out of a portfolio or printed by a customer and expected to adhere exactly to the original), leaning instead toward designs that require careful sketches from the artist and a great deal of creative work. Artists (and front-of-house employees) at these parlors may have little patience for beginners, but they're certainly reputable professionals; they just don't specialize in four-leaf clovers and kanji.

But what if teens *don't* visit reputable parlors?

Whether or not your teen patrons mention it, they may be thinking of going to an amateur for a tattoo or piercing. Whether operating out of a van or someone's living room, these "artists" have the questionable appeal of not asking for parental consent— a legal requirement for anyone wishing to tattoo or pierce a minor; nearly every state with body modification laws on the books specifies fines or criminal penalties otherwise. Remind teens that if they don't see clearly visible certificates on the wall, they're putting themselves at risk. Amateur artists may not use clean needles or bother wearing gloves—leading to mild infection at best, or at worst, anything from hepatitis to HIV from the last body to touch the needles.

If the threat of infection doesn't scare off teens, the threat of a bad tattoo or mangled piercing certainly should. Any unlicensed "professional" may not have had any formal training, and almost certainly didn't go through the apprenticeship process most parlors (and, indeed, many state laws and regulations) require. While it's possible that untrained artists and piercers can produce the same high-quality results as their fully licensed peers, the truth is that quality tattoos and consistent piercings don't just happen through sheer force of will; they're the result of long hours of training and practice. Amateur tattoos may be asymmetrical, wobbly, inconsistent in color, and fade more easily than professional tattoos. Amateur piercings may be asymmetrical or improperly placed, increasing the risk of nerve damage or hitting a vein. Both come with increased risk of infection and complications in healing.

Teens under 18 who have obtained parental consent (or those able to consent for themselves) may still have no idea where to go for a tattoo or piercing, or may only be interested in their cheapest option. You don't have to recommend any venue in particular, but do tell them a few things to look for in a tattoo or piercing parlor:

- **Staff who are available to talk.** Either venue should have artists or staff available for simple consultation before getting any work done. If a shop is used to quickly getting paperwork signed and fitting in customer after customer, assembly-line style, teens may feel rushed into a decision they will later regret. First-time customers may also have a poor experience if they stop at a parlor similar to the ones mentioned previously, where artists primarily work with experienced customers. Teens should never stay in a parlor or shop where they feel rushed or disrespected.
- **Cleanliness.** The shop should also be extremely clean; even unwashed floors can contribute to risk of infection, and untidiness in the front of the shop may reflect lack of hygiene in the work areas. State licensing and regulating authorities assess cleanliness as part of their inspections as well, so a dirty shop

may indicate a license that's not up-to-date. It's a little like the restaurant industry and the health department; regulators should be touring facilities often and unannounced. Shops should also have clean and well-functioning restrooms available to their customers, and allow breaks whenever needed by the artist or customer.

- **Proper documentation.** A licensed shop or parlor should ask for a driver's license or other government identification, which they should then photocopy for their own records. (Teens who visit the same shop multiple times may not have to relinquish their ID each time, although the front-of-house staff will likely ask them to produce it.) Most states allow teens under 18 to get a tattoo or piercing with parental consent, although some don't allow work on anyone under 16 regardless of parental consent. Some states require only written consent, while others require the consenting parent or guardian to be present at the time of piercing or tattooing. Teens should keep in mind that individual shops and parlors may actually have *more* restrictive policies than the governing city or state, so it's always a good idea for teens who are under 18 to check with individual shops first. Even in a state allowing teens over 16 to get a tattoo or piercing without parental consent, many shops may unilaterally refuse to work on minors.

- **Aftercare.** The staff should have aftercare information readily available to anyone, ideally in writing; many shops will even permanently post aftercare tips and general care suggestions. Some shops have their own branded merchandise for healing, but don't let an artist convince you that you have to buy anything additional from them; adequate aftercare supplies for both tattoos and piercings can be purchased over the counter at any drugstore. While a piercing doesn't usually require any bandaging or healing supplies right out of the shop, a new tattoo should be thoroughly cleaned and covered with a sterile bandage for anywhere from an hour to several hours, depending on the size and complexity of the piece; a tattoo artist should provide this bandage along with tape or an adhesive to keep it on when the piece is finished.

If a teen doesn't start the conversation with you until after the work has been done, you can still help him or her maintain a healthy tattoo or body piercing. Although reputable artists and piercers will send customers home with clear, thorough aftercare information, not all teens will listen to this advice—or visit a reputable professional in the first place. They may read the aftercare information (or not) and then lose it or throw it away. Some of the same advice holds for treating both tattoos and piercings:

- **Wash it.** This one might seem like a no-brainer, but some teens may think that they shouldn't touch a new tattoo or piercing at all, even to clean it. Tattoos should be gently washed with antibacterial soap several times a day following the initial tattooing. Piercings should be washed with the same, but no more often than a usual showering regimen. Never scrub either; aggressive scrubbing can cause irritation or even damage a freshly healing tattoo. Never use abrasive cleaners such as ammonia or cleaners containing alcohol because these can cause great pain and damage the skin.

- **Don't use the good sheets.** Many teens don't know that a new tattoo will "bleed" ink and/or plasma in its first few days. (On the day of the tattoo, this mixture will also include some blood from the use of the tattooing needle.) This is perfectly natural, and won't diminish the final quality of the healed tattoo. The seepage is only excess ink from the tattoo and plasma from the impacted skin, and it's a sign of a healing tattoo. It should slow down and stop altogether after a few days, depending on the size and complexity of the piece. In the meantime, teens will want to use sheets and clothing that they don't mind getting dirty; tattoo ink can stain many fabrics when it's fresh. If the seepage turns bloody after the first day, or if any discolored discharge appears, seek medical attention immediately.

- **Treat it.** In the first few days of a new tattoo, A+D ointment should be applied to the washed tattoo. Once the tattoo has stopped losing ink and starts to scab or flake, switch to a low-alcohol lotion applied (with clean hands) as needed. (Some studios disagree on proper treatment; many artists recommend starting with an ointment and then moving to a lotion, while others, particularly those who formulate their own aftercare lotion, may start off directly with a lotion. Either practice is acceptable, and teens who get more than one tattoo may grow to prefer one method over the other regardless of what a particular parlor or artist recommends.) Washing the tattoo and applying lotion should soothe the itching or burning sensation that often accompanies a new piece. The tattoo itself may also feel raised above the surrounding skin while it's healing; this should subside as the tattoo heals, but teens with any skin condition—particularly one that may have implications for scarring and healing—should consult with a doctor and a reputable tattoo artist before getting any work done. The area around a new tattoo may also swell slightly (or significantly, depending on the size of the piece) as the body increases blood flow to the area to heal the wound and prevent infection. A tattoo that stays swollen for several days or starts out normal and swells several days into the healing process may be infected, and its owner should seek medical attention.

- **Sanitize it.** A new piercing can be sprayed with a simple saline solution, which will soothe the itching sensation that often comes with a new stud or hoop. Teens shouldn't just try to wash with saltwater; part of the efficacy of a saline spray is in its high-velocity delivery. For both a tattoo and piercing, any crust or scabs that form should be rinsed away gently, but never forced off of the skin; scrubbing a scabbed tattoo too soon can actually remove ink and damage the quality of the piece, as well as risk reopening wounds and injuring the skin.

- **Let it breathe.** Tattoo artists send their customers home with the new tattoo in a bandage, which should stay on for a few hours, depending on size. (If the artist says two hours, he or she doesn't mean twenty minutes!) Once this initial dressing is removed, the tattoo shouldn't be covered with a bandage or plastic wrap; the tattoo—essentially an open wound—needs air to heal. The same is true of a new piercing. It may be covered for a short period of time, for instance, during a sports game, where jewelry would ordinarily be removed. (Removing a new piercing with the intention of replacing it increases the risk of infection, and the piercing may actually begin to close.) However, the piercing shouldn't be covered for an extended period. Depending on the location of a tattoo, it may be difficult for a teen to keep it uncovered (at least by clothing) all the time. Teens should be mindful that a healing tattoo—along with being potentially inky and covered in ointment or lotion—can be sticky. Textured fabrics can latch on to the healing tattoo and potentially come away with part of it. Particularly while a tattoo is still scabbing, teens should be mindful of the kinds of clothing they wear. If it sticks to a tattoo or scab, it could potentially pull out part of the tattoo altogether, both increasing the risk of pain and infection as well as damaging the artwork itself.
- **Don't touch it.** New tattoos and piercings should never be touched by unwashed hands. Teens may want to show off the work to their friends, but they shouldn't let their friends handle the area. Unnecessary movement of a new piercing can increase the risk of infection (which is why many piercers will initially put in a stud, which moves less, even when a client hopes to ultimately wear a ring) and new tattoos are so vulnerable to bacteria that they shouldn't be subjected to swimming pools or hot tubs—no matter how good they might feel. Teens should never replace the initial jewelry before a piercing has healed; it's never a bad idea to go back to your piercer if the original jewelry is uncomfortable, or if you think you've healed enough to make the switch to a different design or metal.
- **Use the right jewelry.** Because some parts of the body can swell when pierced, teens may need longer or larger jewelry for the first few weeks or even months. This is particularly true in blood-rich areas, such as the lips or tongue. Teens will eventually know exactly what size or gauge their jewelry is, but a piercer should always be willing to size any jewelry already in the body (so that a teen can purchase the same size in a different metal or design, or a smaller or larger size as needed). Teens should never try to stretch a new piercing (putting in a larger size gauge than was originally inserted, which can be painful) before it has completely healed.
- **Protect it from the sun.** Teens should always wear sunscreen to protect from the harmful effects of the sun's rays, but tattoos in particular are vulnerable to sun damage and should always be covered with sunscreen if they're in a location that will see sun. Teens brandishing a new tattoo while they're still healing

should use a lotion that also includes a sunscreen (besides being low-alcohol or alcohol-free, for comfort). Unprotected tattoos are more likely to fade, and a tattoo—like any part of the body—can be sunburnt. A burn feels particularly painful on top of a recent tattoo, and many after-sun lotions or balms contain chemicals too harsh to expose to a still-healing tattoo.

- **Don't hide it.** It's also important for teens to know the signs of infection and contact information for both their tattoo artist or piercer, and a medical professional who understands the risks of body modification. Many teens, especially those who may have had work done without authentic parental consent, may be afraid to show a tattoo or piercing to a doctor for fear that they'll get in trouble. Admittedly, some doctors do consider body modification risky or unhealthy, and may advise removing the piercing across the board—or lecture the teen, when all he or she wanted was help. That's why it's all the more important for teens to have a relationship with a doctor or nurse they trust. Teens who are considering body modification should bring the topic up with their doctor during a routine checkup, so they know how the conversation would go should an emergency arise. (This is just one of the reasons that teens should consider asking to see a nurse or doctor who specializes in teens, rather than a standard pediatrician, and to be able to speak to that medical professional alone. Teens are more likely to ask questions when their parents aren't in the room, and when they know that their autonomy is respected.)

Even if teens in your library don't know to ask you about tattoos or piercings, you can help them make informed decisions with your collection and resources. If your library website has a section on teen health (and it should!) you can include links to the FDA's statement on tattoos (U.S. Food and Drug Administration, 2011) and the Mayo Clinic's overviews of piercings and tattoos (Mayo Clinic Staff, 2010a, 2010b). Teens researching tattoos and piercings for school purposes will be well served by nonfiction books such as *Tattooing: Tattoos in Modern Society* (Levy, 2009) and *Body Marks: Tattooing, Piercing, and Scarification* (Gay and Whittington, 2002). Teens considering getting a tattoo or piercing themselves, however, are looking less for balanced arguments than for inspiration. For these teens, consider expanding your fine arts collection to include such titles as *The Mammoth Book of Tattoos* (Hardy, 2009), *Tattoo Bible, Book One* and *Book Two* (Superior Tattoo, 2009, 2010), and *Great Book of Tattoo Designs* (Irish, 2007). Periodicals can also be a great help to body modification–minded teens. If you're wary of buying trade publications that amount to little more than catalogs with nice pictures, consider titles such as *Inked*, which features sections on music and fashion, or *Tattoo Flash*, which focuses intensely on artwork and prides itself on a complete lack of advertisements. It is noteworthy that the tattoo industry is still significantly male-dominated, and the covers of many tattoo publications seem to reflect that reality, featuring scantily clad, heavily tattooed women. These covers, however, are no more risqué than a title such as *Rolling Stone*, which is frequently carried in teen areas (and certainly read by teens wherever it may be housed).

Whatever your personal feelings about tattoos and piercings, many of the teens you serve think about them, want them, and may even aspire to create them for a living themselves. Is your library a friendly space for these budding artists and future parlor customers? Even something as small as how you and your staff dress can play a part in indicating to teens that you're open—or closed—to certain conversations. Here are some tips for opening the lines of dialogue:

- **Roll up your sleeves.** If you have tattoos in locations that can reasonably be showed off, why not do it? Teen patrons (and adult patrons, for that matter) won't necessarily admire the work you had done, but they'll certainly notice it. They may not have any adult role models in their lives who have tattoos. They may also be holding on to antiquated stereotypes of tattoos—that only criminals and troublemakers have them, that "good girls" don't have tattoos—that you could squelch.

- **Be honest.** Got a piercing you regretted and took out a month later? Still cringing over that tattoo of your ex's name? Teens need to know that the decisions they make today will still be with them down the line, for better or worse. It's unrealistic to tell teens they shouldn't get tattoos, but it's fair to try to help them avoid mistakes you made. It's also important to be honest about the pain and care involved. Teens who get tattoos and piercings are making an investment that will be written on their bodies. The more care and thought they put into those investments, the more likely they are to stay healthy *and* happy.

- **Don't overshare.** Teens don't need to know that you have a nipple ring, or that you got a tattoo in a . . . sensitive area. It's okay to have boundaries when it comes to talking to teens. You can still speak from experience about the pain involved, how you decided on a location or jewelry, and why aftercare is important—even if you don't reveal all your secrets.

- **Don't judge.** You may have your own standards for what you will and won't put on your body. Teens do, too—they just might be very different standards. Remember that you're not there to impose a moral compass on your teens, no matter what you (or their parents) might think. Try to think about tattoos and piercings like books. You might not like them all, but you don't have to—you just have to help your teens find the right ones.

References

Gay, Kathleen, and Whittington, Christine. 2002. *Body Marks: Tattooing, Piercing, and Scarification*. Brookfield, CT: Twenty-First Century Books.

Hardy, Lal, ed. 2009. *The Mammoth Book of Tattoos*. Philadelphia: Running Press.

Irish, Lora S. 2007. *Great Book of Tattoo Designs*. East Petersburg, PA: Fox Chapel.

Levy, Janey. 2009. *Tattooing: Tattoos in Modern Society*. New York: The Rosen Publishing Group.

Mayo Clinic Staff. 2010a. "Piercings: How to Prevent Complications." Mayo Clinic. February 16. http://www.mayoclinic.com/health/piercings/SN00049.

————. 2010b. "Tattoos: Understand Risks and Precautions." Mayo Clinic. February 16. http://www.mayoclinic.com/health/tattoos-and-piercings/MC00020.

Superior Tattoo. 2009. *Tattoo Bible: Book One*. Stillwater, MN: ArtKulture.

————. 2010. *Tattoo Bible: Book Two*. Stillwater, MN: ArtKulture.

U.S. Food and Drug Administration. 2011. "Tattoos & Permanent Makeup." U.S. Department of Health & Human Services. Last updated April 14. http://www.fda.gov/cosmetics/product andingredientsafety/productinformation/ucm108530.htm.

6

"You Won't Tell Anyone, Right?"— Dating Violence and Abuse

Defining Dating Violence and Abuse

The Centers for Disease Control and Prevention defines teen dating violence as a kind of intimate partner violence that may fit into any of three categories: physical (any kind of physical harm—pinching, hitting, shoving, kicking), emotional (threatening a partner or harming their sense of self-worth through name-calling, shaming, bullying, intentionally embarrassing, or isolating from friends and family), or sexual (forcing a partner to perform any sex act without consent or when they cannot consent, including manipulating or limiting access to birth control) (Centers for Disease Control and Prevention, 2012). A 2008 Liz Claiborne survey found that a distressing number of both teens and tweens (youth ages 11–14) have experienced dating violence or know someone who has. According to the survey, among teens who have had sex by age 14, 69 percent have been through at least one form of dating abuse, including one in three who have been physically abused by a partner (Liz Claiborne, 2008).

Another Claiborne study looked specifically at technology use within teen relationships, and found more disturbing results:

- One in three teens who've been in a relationship say they've been texted up to *30 times an hour* by a partner to find out where they are, who they're with, or what they're doing.
- One in four have been called names, put down, or harassed by a partner via text or phone.
- One in five have been asked by Internet or phone to engage in sexual activity when they didn't want to.
- Nearly one in five say a partner has used the Internet or a cell phone to spread a rumor about them.
- Seventeen percent say a partner made them afraid not to respond to a text or call.

49

- One in ten were threatened physically via text, chat, instant message (IM), or e-mail
- Sixteen percent say a partner bought them cell phone minutes.

Additionally, a high majority of teens don't tell their parents about these behaviors, even though both teens and parents (51 percent and 58 percent, respectively) believe cell phones and other technologies make dating abuse more likely, and easier to keep hidden (48 percent and 53 percent) (Liz Claiborne, 2007).

Why is teen dating violence and abuse so common? Abusers themselves may be more depressed or aggressive than their peers, but other risk factors include exposure to trauma, alcohol abuse, lack of parental supervision, or acquaintance with others who are in abusive relationships (Centers for Disease Control and Prevention, 2012). As for their victims, while high numbers of teens—even very young teens—have experience with dating violence or abuse (62 percent of tweens who have been in a relationship have friends who have been verbally abused, while 20 percent of 13- to 14-year-olds know someone who has been struck by a boyfriend or girlfriend), many of them (51 percent of tweens) don't know the warning signs of abuse, or where to go for help if someone they know is being abused (54 percent of tweens) (Liz Claiborne, 2008).

Abusive relationships revolve around power and control. These relationships may cycle between three phases: a period of tension, often one provoked by the abuser; a violent outburst; and a sort of "honeymoon" phase, where the abuser apologizes for their behavior and makes the victim feel loved and cherished. While no two abusive relationships are alike, almost all of them are characterized by escalating abuse and violence (Break the Cycle, 2009). Here are ten common warning signs for abuse, as listed by Break the Cycle, a national nonprofit organization addressing teen dating violence:

- **Checking partner's cell phone or e-mail without permission.** An abuser is inherently distrustful of his partner. (Although teen abusers, like adult abusers, are more likely to be male, both young men and women may be perpetrators of violence. Dating violence may take place in heterosexual or homosexual relationships. In this chapter I alternate pronouns deliberately to acknowledge that anyone may be the victim of dating violence or abuse.) He forces her to prove her fidelity and account for her whereabouts at all times. He may check text messages, call histories, or e-mail conversations for ammunition against his partner, or even send messages disguised as his victim to isolate her from family and friends. If the abuser purchases cell phone minutes for his victim (by paying the contract directly, offering money for minutes used beyond a contract, or purchasing a pre-paid phone), he may use this as leverage to justify monitoring the victim's mobile activities. The abuser may also *remove* things from his victim's phone: contacts, text messages, histories. He may do this to attempt to limit his partner's contact with the outside world or to erase evidence of his meddling. Both victim and abuser may delete texts and calls in order to hide their activities from parents or other concerned adults.

- **Constant put-downs.** An abuser destroys her partner's self-confidence and makes him dependent on her by convincing her partner that he is ugly, stupid, and unlovable. The abuser may even begin using these put-downs as nicknames, constantly reminding her partner of his (perceived) failings. A victim may stay with his partner in part because he has been so thoroughly brainwashed into believing only the abuser would want to be with him. While friends and loved ones may question this perpetual stream of insults, the victim often asserts that his partner is "only joking," convincing outsiders that the words are only friendly teasing. Once again, the victim feels forced to defend his own abuser to those who might actually be able to help.

- **Extreme jealousy or insecurity.** As much as an abuser may feed on his victim's insecurities, he will also broadcast his own, using jealousy and insecurity as reasons to keep his partner isolated from others. He will insist that he would be too lonely without his partner, or even threaten to hurt himself if the partner goes away. The smallest words or deeds may provoke his jealousy, framing all other friends or acquaintances as potential rivals. Interaction with any other male—even teachers, gay friends, or adults—sparks the abuser to accuse his partner of infidelity, forcing her to choose between her friends (and even acquaintances) and him. Of course, the "choice" isn't really a choice—the abuser will do just about anything to keep his victim firmly under his control.

- **Explosive temper.** The smallest perceived slights may set off rages and tantrums. Minor inconveniences that might leave anyone else simply frustrated leave an abuser enraged. Above all, the abuser convinces her partner that these outbursts are the *victim's* fault, that the abuser simply cannot help herself when "provoked" by her partner. These outbursts may be disguised if the abuser is involved in sports, where tempers run high when fueled by competition (and testosterone), but the victim quickly gets used to navigating the minefield of his partner's moods and rages. Anger that starts with raised voices may quickly escalate to property destruction, thrown objects, and physical abuse or altercations.

- **Financial control.** While adult abusers may take over joint bank accounts or investments, younger abusers may simply insist on always paying for meals or outings (or, indeed, cell phone minutes), building up precedent for telling the victim she "owes" him something—love, loyalty, sex. Indeed, an abuser may even lure a potential partner with lavish gifts and expensive meals if these are luxuries the victim could not afford on her own. The abuser may also lead the victim into accruing debt—say, promising to pay her way through college, and then withdrawing financial support partway through the semester. This financial dependency is designed to further cut off the victim from the outside world and to establish outsiders as financially demanding, while the abuser can "protect" his victim and keep her under his watchful eye.

- **Isolation from family and friends.** One of the easiest ways to keep a victim dependent on his abuser—and ensure that no one else knows what is truly going on in the relationship—is to isolate him from anyone else who might care about him. Teens in particular may simply believe their friend is too busy being in a couple to hang out or talk, and indeed this often seems to be the reality in many new adolescent relationships. But in nonabusive relationships, the "honeymoon" wears off and teens remember their friends and the other activities they used to enjoy before becoming part of a couple. The all-encompassing aspects of "young love" relationships may keep outsiders from discovering the truth. Keeping a partner away from her close friends and family members also means keeping her away from anyone she might trust enough to listen to when they express their concerns about the abuser.

- **Mood swings.** The abuser is kind and loving one minute and snarling with rage the next. She keeps her partner off-balance with constantly shifting, unpredictable moods. Her partner's life suddenly revolves around trying to keep the abuser happy, as if his actions actually had any impact on the abuser's mood. This may actually serve to further isolate her partner, as she may successfully convince him that his friends (or family, or school, or anything else standing in the way of the abusive relationship) are the ones who provoke her intense moods. The fleeting moments of happiness, when the abuser is suddenly all smiles and charm, make the inevitable rages and tantrums all the more jarring, but the victim is convinced that if he could only do the "right" thing, say the "right" words, that happiness could be an everyday reality.

- **Physical harm of any kind.** Physical abuse rarely starts with direct physical attacks such as a punch to the face. Instead, it starts small, perhaps with a pinch, rough horseplay, or "playful" swats on the behind. It is benign enough that the victim at first convinces herself that nothing is wrong, that the physicality is simply different from other relationships she has known. An abuser will often mock his partner for being too sensitive if she complains, or ignore her requests to be gentler. Soon she is convinced that she *is* being too sensitive, that the touches must not be as bad as they seem. These milder forms of violence will eventually give way to more forceful attacks, especially the kind that leave unseen marks. Many abusers know exactly where to apply force so that their blows sting and ache for days, but remain unseen to anyone outside the relationship. They also know their victims will be too scared to show anyone the bruises, cuts, or welts. This kind of physical abuse may also lead to rough or forced sex. Victims may consent to sex but not to the sexual acts their partners demand, or may consent to sex but not to violent sex that leaves them injured and sore (with wounds on the inside, where *no one* will see them). Victims may also initially object to sex, but give in when they realize the "choice" is between sex or injury. As with instances of sexual assault, the body may betray the mind, leaving the victim deeply ashamed of the sexual encounter yet convinced that they enjoyed it on some level. Abusers reinforce this notion by insisting the sex was consensual and that the partner liked it.

- **Possessiveness.** An abuser seeks to own her victim. She may start out charmingly, insisting that she simply doesn't want to share her partner with others or pouting when her partner makes other plans, but ultimately the abuser seeks control over her partner's schedule, relationships, and body. Initially this kind of possessiveness can be flattering, particularly for a partner with low self-esteem, but eventually the abuser forces her victim to choose her over friends, family, school—anything in the victim's life that is *not* controlled by the abuser.

- **Telling a partner what to do.** An abuser may start out by offering "suggestions," but these quickly give way to coercion. He will sulk and give his partner the silent treatment whenever he doesn't get his way. Temper tantrums may end with the *victim* apologizing. Ultimately the abuser gives orders, and doles out punishment if these orders aren't followed—or if he *thinks* they weren't. The abuser gives ultimatums frequently and leaves his victim convinced that going against his wishes will lead to abandonment or violence.

While these should all be warning signs to teens who are in relationships, not all the signs may be apparent to those *outside* the relationship—including adults like you. You may interact with teens as couples, but it's also possible you have a relationship only with the victim, who may (intentionally or unintentionally) show signs of abuse:

- **Change in affect.** A once outgoing, talkative, and confident teen who withdraws socially and engages less in library activities may be responding to pressure from an abuser. Even if the boyfriend or girlfriend isn't yet isolating the teen from friends and family, dealing with an emotionally volatile partner may make many teens shut down, physically and mentally exhausted. Look for teens whose moods no longer match their surroundings, who offer little in the way of emotional expression, or who seem to flinch at the sign of any kind of conflict. Teens coping with an abusive partner may start to interpret *all* relationships as potential minefields. They may play peacemaker when they see arguments develop, or they may seem physically impacted by raised voices and physical gestures.

- **Physical signs.** Bruises, scratches, or cuts may be signs of self-harm—or of a teen in an abusive relationship. Many abusers are careful not to leave marks that can't be easily covered, rather than risk alerting friends or adults, but those who can't control their temper may not be so careful. Teens may conceal their injuries around other adults, but "accidentally" show them off when they're around an adult they trust. The victim may also be embarrassed about the injuries or try to downplay them, attempting to convince others that they're not truly hurt. Listen for changing stories or vague explanations ("I fell down"), particularly from teens you know to be usually cautious and coordinated.

- **Excusing partner's behavior.** Listen for mentions of a teen's partner that are quickly followed by excuses: "He's not usually like that." "This is the first time it's happened." "She's just a little jealous, that's all." Teens may even ask *you* if their partner's behavior is normal—and backpedal immediately if you say it's not: "Oh, well, I mean, he didn't get *that* mad." "She would never hurt me on purpose." They're trying to normalize the relationship, to convince you (just as much as themselves) that what's going on is perfectly normal.

- **Taking refuge in the library.** Teens who don't feel safe may try to keep themselves in public places as much as possible, to avoid being alone with an abusive partner. Watch out for teens who make excuses for why they *need* to be in the library, particularly if a partner tries to get them to leave. If you're concerned about a teen leaving with a partner, be discreet: tell the partner you need the teen's help with a special project, that there's a phone call for the teen—anything to get the teen to a private place where you can discuss finding another ride home and possibly going to the authorities.

- **Not wanting to leave.** A teen who is too afraid to tell you they're being abused may nonetheless give you nonverbal cues when the abusive partner (or family member) comes to retrieve them from the library. Watch for a teen's posture and body language to change, as well as other signs of stress like a racing pulse or shortness of breath. A teen who doesn't ordinarily participate in library programs may suddenly express interest in staying for your gaming tournament, or suddenly offer to help shelve books.

- **Seeking information on abuse.** Of course, not all teens who want to read about abuse are being abused, just as not all teens who look for information about sex or drugs have any experience with either. But teens who frequently seek out themes of abuse, especially if they want specific legal information, may be researching a real situation rather than a general interest. These teens may ask "hypothetical" questions, or test the waters with an "I know someone who . . ." story. They're gauging your reaction to the topic, and trying to get help without admitting that they need it. Always treat hypothetical questions as if they're real, and be gentle with teens who are having trouble admitting that the "friend" in question is right in front of you.

At this point it's prudent to remember that, particularly if you work in a school environment, you do have a responsibility to report abuse or suspected abuse. As we learned in the chapter on homelessness, mandatory reporting doesn't have to be an intimidating or frightening concept; it's a policy designed to help the teens you serve and keep them safe. If you're ever concerned that a teen might be in danger or may have already been hurt by a partner or family member, or if a teen tells you directly that this has occurred, your responsibility is to make sure that the "secret" doesn't stay hidden with you. Talk to a coworker, a supervisor, a social worker, or a nurse—anyone who may have insight into the situation and know the best next step. Don't think that *you* need to be the one immediately calling the Department of Social Services or that you'll single-handedly have to protect a teen from an abusive partner. Your job is to be a trustworthy adult.

Part of earning your teens' trust is treating their relationships as real and valid, even if you believe they aren't healthy. You may see a teen playing into destructive patterns of abuse and enabling, but telling her that only broadcasts that you don't approve of her choices. Remember that a teen is already putting herself into a vulnerable position by admitting what's going on in her relationship—especially to an adult—and the way you react to this information may determine whether or not she ever comes back to you.

Key phrases to avoid:

- "How could you let him/her do this to you?"
- "Why are you staying with him/her?"
- "You should have known better."
- "Did you do something to provoke him/her?"

Good phrases to remember:

- "This isn't your fault."
- "Relationships don't have to hurt."
- "You deserve a partner who loves and supports you."

Perhaps your most important duty as a trusted and trustworthy adult is to *listen*. This may be the first time many teens have told an adult, or *anyone*, about what's going on in their relationship. They're looking for signs that you're paying attention and that you care about the information they're sharing. If ever there was a time *not* to multitask when talking with a teen, this is it. Put down the book, turn away from the screen, and *listen*. Listening may also mean not offering input at first; a teen who confides in you may initially just want to unload. No doubt it will frustrate or stress you out to hear painful details about a teen's relationship and then not be able to offer insight or help, but be patient; if you listen well, that teen will come back to you.

In the meantime, continue the conversation with other trustworthy adults. If you've seen a teen in distress, or if you know that a teen shouldn't leave the building with a noncustodial parent or a potentially abusive partner, let other coworkers and security guards know. You don't have to share the details with everyone; just calmly explain that a teen has made his wishes clear. You can't deny anyone entry without a restraining order if they haven't violated library rules, but you can certainly ask anyone who causes a disturbance to leave, and make it clear that no one else has to leave *with* them.

It's also important to be in close contact with other adults and organizations in your community who can provide support to abused teens. Know the resources for battered women and families, as well as any organizations dedicated to LGBT victims of violence. Find out whether teens in your state can file restraining orders, or whether they need an adult guardian. Does your community have emergency shelters for abused teens, or drop-in centers that may cater to other populations (such as homeless youth) but offer potential resources to abused teens? Have contact information for the Department of Social Services or any youth welfare agencies in your area close at hand. As we discussed in the chapter on homeless teens, it's a good idea to start a dialogue with these organizations *before* you have real teens in mind. Aside from ensuring that you'll probably have a more level head for the conversation, starting when you're not in crisis mode also means you'll know what warning signs would require the police or other agencies to take action, rather than mentioning a teen or family by name and later realizing you didn't have all the information.

You can also consider the library and library resources a part of the recovery process for teens who have been abused. Let them know that the library is a safe space, and that you can offer them access to any information they need, without question or judgment. You may want to offer these teens an opportunity to get more involved in library programs and activities. Invite them to join your teen advisory group. Let them participate in volunteer activities, such as shelving or processing books. If your library has a children's section, see if the children's librarian might let them do storytime or crafts with younger children. All these activities can help abuse victims regain confidence and reestablish their sense of self, both of which may have been badly damaged by a violent or abusive relationship.

In providing library materials for teens who may be experiencing or concerned about dating violence or abuse, remember to stock both fiction and nonfiction titles. Although its ending may be a bit simplistic, *Bitter End* (Brown, 2011) offers a highly realistic depiction of a teenage girl, Alex, who becomes entangled in a relationship with the manipulative and possessive Cole. Particularly striking are the depictions of Alex's best friends, who quickly pick up on Cole's temper and other warning signs, and an older coworker who offers Alex support.

You should also make sure your library's website offers ample electronic resources. Link to any local or state organization and list hotlines or anonymous tip lines. Provide contact information for the police department (including nonemergency lines to local stations), shelters for battered women and families, sexual and mental health clinics, your local Department of Social Services or its equivalent, and any applicable counseling or therapeutic resources. Many colleges and universities offer confidential help lines for victims of sexual assault or even simple peer help lines; find out if any of your local schools offer services to teens as well.

While it's important to offer all this information on your library website, it's also vital to offer these resources—particularly phone numbers—where teens can be sure to read them alone. Post these numbers clearly and frequently in restrooms. A teen who can't look at anything on a computer without an abusive boyfriend or girlfriend watching over his or her shoulder may at least be able to jot down a number if they see it in a bathroom stall.

Highly Recommended Resources

- **Love Is Respect** (http://www.loveisrespect.org/)
  Created by Liz Claiborne, Love Is Respect seeks to inform teens about the reality of dating violence and abuse and offer resources to learn more and get help.
- **Break the Cycle** (http://www.breakthecycle.org/)
  A national nonprofit dedicated to breaking the cycle of youth domestic violence, Break the Cycle offers multiple sets of resources to different audiences—including teens. Their teen-specific site, http://www.thesafespace.org/, integrates a number of social media tools and is soliciting app developers to create apps to fight abuse.
- **The Hotline—The National Domestic Violence Hotline** (1.800.799.SAFE) (http://www.thehotline.org/)
  This website offers a variety of resources for domestic abuse victims, including information geared specifically for teens and for immigrants.

References

Break the Cycle. 2009. "Dating Violence 101." Break the Cycle. Accessed August 28, 2011. http://www.breakthecycle.org/dating-violence-101.

Brown, Jennifer. 2011. *Bitter End*. New York: Little, Brown and Company.

Centers for Disease Control and Prevention. 2012. "Understanding Teen Dating Violence." Centers for Disease Control and Prevention. http://www.cdc.gov/ViolencePrevention/pdf/TeenDatingViolence2012-a.pdf.

Liz Claiborne, Inc. 2007. "Tech Abuse in Teen Relationships Study." LoveIsRespect.org. http://www.loveisrespect.org/wp-content/uploads/2009/03/liz-claiborne-2007-tech-relationship-abuse.pdf.

———. 2008. "Teen and Tween Dating Violence and Abuse Study." LoveIsRespect.org. http://www.loveisrespect.org/wp-content/uploads/2008/07/tru-tween-teen-study-feb-081.pdf.

7

"Does That Get You High?"— Drugs and Alcohol

Teens and Tobacco Products

Each day in the United States, about 4,000 adolescents (young people ages 12 through 17) try their first cigarette (National Center for Chronic Disease Prevention and Health Promotion, 2010a). Teen smoking rates remain stable with about 27 percent of teens reporting smoking in the past month (Feliz, 2011). Forty-six percent of high school students have *ever* tried smoking, including one or two puffs. Eleven percent have smoked an entire cigarette before turning 13. Nearly 9 percent of high school students (15 percent of males and 2 percent of females) use smokeless tobacco (commonly known as chew, snuff, or dip) (National Center for Chronic Disease Prevention and Health Promotion, 2010b). These numbers are particularly alarming when we note that the Centers for Disease Control estimates that the rate of *adult* smoking is only at 21 percent (Centers for Disease Control and Prevention, 2011b). And teens suffer the same ill health effects from tobacco products that their adult counterparts do—if not worse.

Smoking at an early age increases the risk of lung cancer. Cigarette smoking causes heart disease—the leading cause of death in the United States—as well as stroke, lung disease, and cancers of the lung, mouth, pharynx, esophagus, and bladder (cancer and stroke being the second and third leading causes of death, respectively) (Centers for Disease Control and Prevention, 2011a). Smokeless tobacco use also causes its share of cancers (addicts run the risk of later removal of the tongue, jaw, or cheeks, in whole or in part) as well as an increased risk for heart disease and stroke, and gum recession. Cigar smoking also increases the risk of various cancers (National Center for Chronic Disease Prevention and Health Promotion, 2010b).

The younger a person starts smoking cigarettes, the more likely he or she is to become strongly addicted to nicotine. And young people suffer the same withdrawal symptoms as adults when they try to quit. Studies have shown nicotine to be addictive in ways similar to heroin, cocaine, and alcohol—and cigarette smoking is the addictive behavior most likely to start in adolescence. One study showed that 51 percent of high school students who smoke had tried to quit during the last year (National Center for Chronic Disease Prevention and Health Promotion, 2010b). Quitting can also be tough for teens because many of the anti-smoking aids available to adults—such as nicotine patches or gum—can't be legally purchased by anyone under 18. (NicoDerm CQ, one of the most popular nicotine patches available in the United States, offers the disclaimer that even its *website* [http://www.nicodermcq.com/] is intended for those over 18.)

All 50 states have laws on the books prohibiting the sale (or gift) of tobacco to minors, yet one survey found 14 percent of teen smokers under the age of 18 usually got their cigarettes by buying them in a store or gas station (National Center for Chronic Disease Prevention and Health Promotion, 2010b). As with bars and liquor stores, teens know (and spread the word) when a particular location or even a single employee is more lax about asking for identification before selling, and of course older siblings and friends are still more than willing to make a purchase for younger smokers. Youth smoking laws prevent the *sale* of tobacco products to minors, not the *possession* of tobacco products *by* minors—so unlike teens who are caught with alcohol, teens who are busted smoking suffer no consequences unless they're on school grounds and can be disciplined by the school. (Indeed, in keeping with municipal laws about smoking on school property, many schools may now assess applicable fines along with any school disciplinary charges.)

Even teens who don't smoke themselves but hang out with smokers—as well as teens who live in households where another family member smokes—are at risk for new or worsening asthma, respiratory diseases, and even stunted growth of the lungs because the adolescent body is still developing (National Center for Chronic Disease Prevention and Health Promotion, 2010b).

Spotting Teen Smokers

You may think teen smoking is obvious, and indeed many teens *want* to draw attention to their tobacco habits. Many teens make no effort to conceal their smoking, even when it violates school or family rules. If you work in a school library, no doubt you and your colleagues know all too well where students go to have a smoke. They may slip out poorly monitored building exits, hide behind dumpsters or portable classroom trailers, or leave school property altogether and smoke on a public street in full view of the school. They may also try to smoke undiscovered in stairwells, locker rooms, and bathrooms.

Your first step, then, should be finding out for sure where your teens like to smoke, and make those locations less desirable. If you work in a public library the "on school grounds" laws are of little use, but do look up the municipal laws in your state or region and find out if the smoking laws specify how far from building entrances smokers must remain. You can ask security guards to enforce that perimeter and remove trash cans or ashtrays from the sidewalks.

It's also important to get the other adults in your building on board with curbing smoking in and around your library. Your colleagues may think they're being discreet when they themselves go outside to smoke, but teens pay attention to the habits of other smokers. If adult role models are smoking in prohibited areas, why should teens behave any differently?

Spotting teens *while* they smoke may not be difficult, but what about when they come into the library?

- **The smell.** It's usually not hard to find a smoker who's just come in from finishing a butt if you're anywhere downwind of them. The smell of cigarette smoke is distinctive, and it clings to the hair and clothing of anyone who smokes or surrounds themselves with smoke. This means the smell of smoke may be more obvious in colder months, when smokers (and their buddies) are wearing more layers that can take on the scent. Because nonsmokers can also come in smelling of smoke if they stand around while their friends inhale, a more accurate way to pick out the smokers may be the smell of nicotine on the breath. Smoker's breath is almost as distinctive as coffee breath, and over time a smoker will exhale the nicotine scent even when they haven't been smoking recently. Teens in particular may try to freshen their breath to avoid being caught, so keep an eye out for teens who only seem to chew gum or pop a mint when they come in from outside.
- **The color.** Nicotine can discolor the fingertips, particularly among smokers who roll their own cigarettes. Look for slightly yellowed or brownish nails and fingertips. Nicotine can also discolor the teeth, leaving the enamel yellow despite otherwise good oral hygiene. Ultimately a heavy smoker may have an overall yellow or grey pallor.
- **The sound.** New smokers generally cough when trying their first cigarettes, as they aren't yet used to the sensation of pulling smoke into their lungs and exhaling. Regular smokers, at greater risk for asthma and various types of respiratory distress, may develop a habitual cough. If you see teens who smoke outdoors, they may spit frequently to get rid of phlegm. The heaviest smokers may see an effect on their voice, with repeated exposure to smoke irritating the vocal cords and leading to a raspy or scratchy tone.
- **Weight loss.** Many teens start smoking (or go back to smoking after trying to quit) because they believe cigarettes will help them lose weight. Although it's true that the oral fixation that comes with nicotine addiction may lead a quitting smoker to pick up a snack or a drink, the real reason behind weight fluctuations and smoking lies in the metabolic effects of cigarettes. Smoking a cigarette raises the metabolic rate, burning more calories faster—but also raising the

heart rate, beating potentially 10–20 times more per minute. Cigarettes also suppress the appetite, meaning a smoker who quits may experience a marked increase in feelings of hunger (H. Lee Moffitt Cancer Center and Research Institute, 2000). Teens may be sucked into smoking because they believe it's an "easy" way to lose or maintain weight, and it's true—all a smoker has to do is drastically increase their risk of heart disease and cancer, diminish lung capacity, and damage the throat, lungs, and respiratory system. Easy!

- **Decreased athletic ability.** You might think that teens who are athletes would stay away from cigarettes, but unfortunately sports-minded teens are just as likely to smoke as their non-athlete peers. Look for teens who are frequently short of breath, have to stop running or other physical exertion, or decline to participate in events with a lot of movement (even activities such as *Dance Dance Revolution*) that they used to enjoy. The loss of stamina and respiratory difficulties that come with smoking may be the culprit.

- **The buzz.** Nicotine does produce a small "high," which many smokers depend on to stay up late or work long shifts. Unfortunately the power of that high diminishes the longer a person smokes—just as the high from other drugs fades away—often leading smokers to consume more and more cigarettes just to get the same impact. Look for teens who seem to have dramatic mood swings or changes in productivity—listless one moment, energized the next—or those who seem particularly irritable at regular intervals (usually indicating that they haven't yet had a nicotine fix).

- **The residue.** For all its other health and social ills, smoking is also the most widely accepted form of littering. Smokers may dispose of their butts in trash cans or butt receptacles, or they may simply dump them wherever they wish— out car windows, on sidewalks, dumped en masse in parking lots. Aside from being a safety hazard (butts thrown out of windows can hit bystanders or other motorists, and still-burning embers from cigarettes can be extreme fire hazards), the litter can help you figure out who your smokers are. Pay attention to when butts appear outside your library, and keep an eye out for empty cartons or the cellophane wrapping that comes on new packs. For the smokeless tobacco users, look for discolored areas on your sidewalks or in mulch or flower beds. Those who chew or dip may also use aluminum cans or water bottles so that they can spit (relatively) inconspicuously indoors. If your building doesn't have vending machines (or doesn't sell sugary drinks such as sodas), keep an eye out for teens who always seem to have a Diet Coke can on them. Litterbugs may even leave their cans or bottles behind, which will have a distinctive smell and look: the scent is similar to the stench of habitual cigarette smoke, and "used" smokeless tobacco is brown, wet, and slightly fibrous. (Think used tea leaves, but grosser.)

How to Stop Smokers

Identifying the smokers who use your library may be easy, but dissuading them from smoking altogether isn't. You'll probably have some success keeping the actual cigarettes away from prohibited areas (particularly if you're in a school with consistent enforcement of tobacco policies, or a library with a strong security or police presence), but convincing teens to give up something they say they like can be tough.

- **Make the health risks real.** If you ask most teen smokers about the risks of smoking, they'll probably rattle off cancer and maybe even heart disease—but they may also believe that because they feel "fine" now, none of those ailments will befall them. If you have a significant teen smoking population, consider using graphic (graphic as in viscerally upsetting, not pie charts) visuals prominently in your library and on the library website. Show a diseased lung. Find a picture of a tobacco user with a tongue or jaw removed. Create infographics on the number of smokers who fall victim to heart disease, lung cancer, and stroke. See if you can get a cancer survivor or another recovering smoker to speak to your teens.
- **Provide alternatives.** Okay, so you can't exactly hand out nicotine patches or gum at the library. Aside from that pesky over-18 thing, products designed to wean smokers off of nicotine aren't cheap. What you *can* provide, however, are other objects that can help teens trying to quit with some of their withdrawal symptoms. Try sugar-free hard candy to help the oral fixation without adding extra calories. Stock up on cheap pens and expect that they'll disappear quickly from your desk; teens will appreciate having something to fiddle with in their hands, and you'll no doubt see a few pens and pencils chewed to death as well. To really provide alternatives to cigarettes, however, you need to know *why* your teens are smoking. If you find you have a lot of teen girls smoking to lose weight, consider adding nutrition groups or safe dieting support as part of your programming. If teens are smoking because they say it relieves stress or helps them relax, think about yoga, meditation, or other relaxation classes at the library. And if teens smoke because they think it looks cool, you need to enlist the help of other teens.
- **Make it uncool.** A lot of adults offering advice to help teens stop smoking will tell you to appeal to teens' vanity. Smoking is gross! You're unattractive when you smoke! The smell, the breath, the cough! But here's the problem with that approach: teens don't smoke so that *you'll* think they're cool. They smoke to make their *peers* think they're cool. If anything, being repulsive to adults is a *bonus* for a lot of teens. I don't want to trot out the tired stereotype that teens are just contrary and rebel against adult society, because that's simply not true all the time. But it *is* true that adults digging in their heels with teens can truly backfire.

It's true that teens want to look good to the adults they admire, so you may make some headway by finding adult role models who don't smoke and are vocal about why. Hollywood has made *some* headway in reducing cigarette smoking in film and television—although historically accurate, cigarettes didn't appear in the ABC show *Pan Am*, because ABC's parent company, Disney, didn't approve—but cigarettes are still ubiquitous on screen, as they are in life. Sports-minded teens may be steered toward images of Major League Baseball, whose leadership has significantly curbed (though not, it should be noted, banned) the use of tobacco products by its players and managers. For every Nick Swisher with an obviously bulging lower lip, there's a Terry Francona stuffing yet another piece of chewing gum into his mouth.

But let's get back to the idea that teens are more easily swayed by one another than by adults. Many of us who aren't doctors or nurses can't understand how so many in the health care profession continue to smoke. Aside from being one of the only guaranteed ways to steal a quick break on an otherwise grueling shift, smoking can be a bonding exercise. Many smokers take intense pride in smoking outside in near-blizzard conditions, toughing it out with their fellow nicotine fiends. Teens are no different. They smoke *together*, with their friends, and even pick up smoking to become a part of a particular group. If you want to make smoking unpopular, find out who *is* popular. Do your teens look up to an older sibling or a leader at their school, like a sports star or class president? Do they have a girlfriend or boyfriend who doesn't smoke and can attest to the displeasing smell and taste of nicotine? Even the health risks you can recite by memory may simply sound more convincing coming out of the mouth of another teen.

It's important to know that you're probably not going to be able to convince every teen who walks through your doors to stop smoking or chewing. You'll be lucky if you can convince *any* of them. Try to remember that the one thing you *can* do is listen—and be honest. If you're a smoker yourself, don't try to hide that from your teens. (They'll find out, trust me.) If you used to smoke and quit, your teens might benefit from hearing what that process was like for you. Was it hard? Did you kick the habit cold turkey, or did you stop gradually? Were you able to quit all at once, or did you get tempted to cheat and have to start all over again? If you've never been a smoker, be honest about your impression of smoking. Do you avoid restaurants or bars with smoking sections? Do you think differently of job applicants if they come in smelling of smoke? Your honesty—more than platitudes, warnings, or threats—may make a teen think twice about tobacco.

Teens and Alcohol

Alcohol is the most popular drug of choice among American teens—more popular than tobacco or other drugs. Although teen alcohol use has decreased in the past two decades, rates are still high at around 42 percent of teens. In 2009, nearly a quarter of teens admitted to binge or occasional heavy drinking (National Center for Chronic Disease Prevention and Health Promotion, 2010a).

Among teens who report alcohol use, more than half (62 percent) had their first full alcoholic drink (not counting sipping or tasting) by age 15. One in four had their first drink by age 12 or *younger*. Almost half of teens (45 percent) don't see a "great risk" in heavy daily drinking, while only 31 percent of teens strongly disapprove of teens and their peers getting drunk (Feliz, 2011). Teens may be blissfully unaware, but excessive alcohol consumption is associated with about 75,000 deaths a year, and alcohol is a factor in more than one-third (41 percent) of all deaths from motor vehicle crashes. Long-term alcohol abuse can lead to liver disease, cancer, cardiovascular disease, and brain damage—not to mention psychiatric issues such as depression, anxiety, and antisocial personality disorder (National Center for Chronic Disease Prevention and Health Promotion, 2010a).

Spotting Teen Drinkers

Adolescents who drink are more likely than their nondrinking peers to develop alcohol problems as adults, but teen drinking has been normalized to the point that 60 percent of teens shrug off the risks with "It's fun to drink" (Feliz, 2011). They see high school parties, drinking at football games, and getting older siblings to buy booze as part and parcel of the adolescent experience. So how can you tell if the teens in your library are among the 42 percent who drink?

- **Physical signs.** Look for teens who are fatigued (particularly those you're used to seeing bright and chipper), who may be nauseated, who have red or glazed eyes, or who have a cough that doesn't seem to go away. All the signs of a hangover that you may remember from your college days or recognize when a colleague overindulges apply to teens, too—and if they're new to drinking, they may not know their own physical limits, which are in flux because their bodies and brains are still developing. You may even see teens while they're still drunk, rather than suffering the next day. In this case, look for teens with a marked lack of motor control, slurred speech, or altered equilibrium. Teen drinkers may try to cover up the smell of alcohol on their breath with gum or mints, but heavy alcohol consumption can assert itself through scent from the pores, not just the mouth or tongue. The smell of heavy drinking is unmistakable, and it doesn't hang on a teen who was merely hanging out with drinkers the way the smell of smoke can.
- **Emotional signs.** Be on the lookout for a teen who has frequent mood swings or sudden personality changes, constant irritability, a drop in self-esteem, poor judgment, depression, or a general lack of interest. Remember that personality or mood changes aren't always negative; a usually introverted, reserved teen who suddenly becomes more social and outgoing should be a concern. It's important

to remember that a teen might not even realize these changes are taking place. If you tell a teen that she seems withdrawn or irritable, her first reaction may be to withdraw even further. A teen who assures you that everything is fine—or who snaps at you just for expressing concern—is definitely one to watch more closely.

- **Family problems.** Teens who were previously model children may withdraw from their parents and siblings, suddenly break family rules, or start arguments with family members. Teens with a family history of alcohol abuse may be particularly at risk for developing a drinking problem themselves (American Academy of Child and Adolescent Psychiatry, 2011), or teens may turn to drinking as a way to cope with existing problems at home. Whatever the reason, a sudden change in the family dynamic should be cause for concern.
- **School problems.** Teens developing a drinking problem may lose interest in school and extracurricular activities, experience a dip in grades (even if they weren't stellar students to begin with), start skipping classes or school altogether, or start having regular discipline problems. If you work at a public library, you're no doubt used to seeing a handful of truants (or several handfuls, depending on your teen population), but you're probably also used to seeing certain hard workers who use the library to do homework or work on school projects. When your overachievers start showing up at the same time as your regular truants, it's time to worry.
- **Social changes.** Look for teens who change their social circle radically, change their personal style drastically (especially those who begin dressing more provocatively, or stop giving as much care to hygiene and appearances), start getting in confrontations with security guards or police, and generally withdraw from the activities and friends they used to enjoy.

How You Can Help

Once you've spotted a teen drinker, how can you help? First, it's important to listen to teens without passing judgment. It's unlikely that a teen will be actively drinking in your library (although it certainly is possible), so you can assure teens that you're not out to call the cops on them. Stress that you want to *help*, because you're worried about the changes you see. Many teens who drink manage to float through adolescence without any adults noticing—or with adults ignoring the issue. Candidly but gently telling a teen that you see many of the signs of alcohol abuse may be the wakeup call they need to take the next step and get medical or psychiatric help.

Other Drugs

One in four teens report taking a prescription drug not prescribed to them by a doctor, and about one in ten have used an over-the-counter cough medicine (for reasons other than soothing a cough) in the past year. Teen ecstasy use rose to 10 percent in 2010 and marijuana use rose to 39 percent. About 10 percent of teens have abused an inhalant, but only 60 percent agree that sniffing or huffing can kill (it can). About 5 percent of teens have used methamphetamine, 4 percent have used heroin, and 9 percent have used cocaine or crack (Feliz, 2011).

Although tobacco is by far teens' drug of choice, harder drugs clearly come with more severe consequences. Drug use contributes (both directly and indirectly) to the HIV epidemic, and a full 50 percent of all deaths to young people ages 15–24 (counting accidents, homicides, and suicides) involve alcohol or drug abuse (American Academy of Child and Adolescent Psychiatry, 2010), which also play a part in physical or sexual aggression (such as assault and rape).

The National Institute on Drug Abuse has thorough information on all commonly abused drugs (National Institute on Drug Abuse, 2011), but it may be useful to acquaint yourself with some of the "highlights." When teens tell you that drugs are fun or that they know how to keep from being addicted, you can remind them that addiction is not the only risk; marijuana can actually impair memory and learning ability, steroids can lead to prostate cancer, and PCP carries the risk of psychosis. Teens may have heard of "acid flashbacks," but LSD actually does carry a risk of hallucinogen persisting perception disorder—a terrifying disorder where hallucinatory flashbacks repeat over and over, interfering with one's work, school, and very grip on reality.

Making the Library Safe for Everyone

Once you've spotted teens who are under the influence of drugs or alcohol—or who admit to you that they've been using—what's the next step? Your goal should be getting these teens the help they need, but also maintaining a library where teens feel safe enough to talk to you about drugs and alcohol, whether they're worried about their own use or that of a friend or loved one.

- **Get everyone on board.** Does your library have a policy in place for how to handle a teen who is actively under the influence of drugs or alcohol? If you're in a school, do you report first to the nurse, to a social worker, or to an administrator? If you're in a public library, would your coworkers call the cops (or security) on a teen who appears high or drunk? Whatever your policy is, make sure everyone sticks to it—and make sure your staff differentiates between adults and teens. There can be a world of difference between a drunk and belligerent adult and a 13-year-old who just tried marijuana for the first time.
- **Reserve judgment.** A teen who comes to you for help won't be inclined to return if your response is all about how irresponsible and stupid it is to do drugs. A teen who merely comes to you for *information* about drugs or alcohol certainly

won't make the leap to asking you for advice if you get all preachy right away. However you feel about drugs, tobacco, and alcohol *personally*, your *professional* responsibility is to make sure that teens have free, easy, and confidential access to whatever information they need—whether that information is the truth about cigarettes and addiction, or contact information for local rehab facilities.

- **Don't punish a Good Samaritan.** It's true that some teens do pull the "I know someone who . . . " card if they don't want to fess up to their own bad behavior, but it's also true that teens worry about their friends and relatives. If you're lucky enough to have gained their trust, these teens may come to you if they think someone in their life needs help. First, don't assume that these teens are using. Knowing a drinker or a drug user doesn't mean the teen telling you is also involved, especially if this is a case of a teen getting into drugs or drinking while they withdraw from old friends. Second, don't press them for the identity of the friend or sibling in trouble; they're likely to think you're just going to get them in more hot water, and they may never come back to you. Trust that if you provide all the information you can and listen respectfully, they'll ultimately reveal the name of the teen in trouble. Teens may feel you out with little detail first to see how you react to the subject; if you freak out, they're gone. Finally, don't punish a teen who's trying to get help for someone else. Many colleges and universities have amnesty policies for students who bring underage friends to get medical help, even if the friends are also underage. These are largely reactions to previous rules that assumed anyone at a party had to be drinking. Students living under those policies were so afraid of punishment from the university that they were less inclined to help a friend—even a friend who may have been suffering from alcohol poisoning. Try to offer amnesty to teens who want to get help for a friend; don't assume they're using, and don't inflict punishments just for helping.

Library Resources and Programs

Pay attention to the way items circulate (or don't circulate) in your library. Do you find that books on drugs or alcohol keep disappearing without being checked out to a particular patron? That's a sure sign that these are touchy subjects in your community. Consider stocking the teen section (and other areas, such as the lobby and restrooms) with brochures about drug use and ways to get help. Does your community have clinics that work with teens, or drop-in centers that may also offer medical screenings and other services? Try to partner with community organizations *other* than the police force. You may find peer counseling particularly effective with teens who may have trouble hearing hard truths about substance abuse from adults. As with other sensitive issues, maintain plenty of resources on the library website.

Ultimately, it's important to remember that you're dealing with teens—teens whose minds and bodies are still developing, and who probably don't know their own brain chemistry well enough to know how a drug will affect them. Teens may not know about drug interaction warnings, and wind up having an adverse reaction to a drug because they were already on medication for asthma or allergies. Teens may also attempt to self-medicate, taking a friend or relative's prescription to try to manage untreated ADHD, depression, undiagnosed pain, or any number of psychiatric issues.

You—and other concerned adults—can help teens be better self-advocates when it comes to their medical care. Many teens (particularly those who participate in sports, and fear that any injury or medical condition would take them away from the game they love) may lie or withhold information when asked by a doctor, particularly if they're worried that what they're experiencing isn't "normal." Teens who are used to being accompanied by a parent to a pediatrician may not feel like they have a voice of their own, or may be afraid to speak up and ask to see a physician specializing in teens or adults. A teen who is comfortable asking *you* for help is more likely to speak candidly with doctors and nurses, too.

References

American Academy of Child and Adolescent Psychiatry. 2010. "Alcohol and Drug Abuse." American Academy of Child and Adolescent Psychiatry. Accessed September 16, 2011. http://www.aacap.org/cs/root/resources_for_families/glossary_of_symptoms_and_illnesses/alcohol_and_drug_abuse.

————. 2011. "Teens: Alcohol and Other Drugs." American Academy of Child and Adolescent Psychiatry. Updated March. http://www.aacap.org/cs/root/facts_for_families/teens_alcohol_and_other_drugs.

Centers for Disease Control and Prevention. 2011a. "Leading Causes of Death." Centers for Disease Control and Prevention. http://www.cdc.gov/nchs/fastats/lcod.htm.

————. 2011b. "Smoking." Centers for Disease Control and Prevention. http://www.cdc.gov/nchs/fastats/smoking.htm.

Feliz, Josie. 2011. "National Study Confirms Teen Drug Use Trending in Wrong Direction: Marijuana, Ecstasy Use Up Since 2008, Parents Feel Ill-Equipped to Respond." The Partnership at Drugfree.org. April 6. http://www.drugfree.org/newsroom/national-study-confirms-teen-drug-use-trending-in-wrong-direction-marijuana-ecstasy-use-up-since-2008-parents-feel-ill-equipped-to-respond.

H. Lee Moffitt Cancer Center and Research Institute. 2000. "Forever Free, Booklet 3—A Guide to Remaining Smoke Free: Smoking and Weight." H. Lee Moffitt Cancer Center and Research Institute at the University of South Florida. Accessed September 19, 2011. http://www.smokefree.gov/pubs/ffree3.pdf.

National Center for Chronic Disease Prevention and Health Promotion. 2010a. "Alcohol & Drug Use." Centers for Disease Control and Prevention. Last modified June 3. http://www.cdc.gov/healthyyouth/alcoholdrug/index.htm.

————. 2010b. "Tobacco Use and the Health of Young People." Centers for Disease Control and Prevention. Last modified June 3. http://www.cdc.gov/healthyyouth/tobacco/facts.htm.

National Institute on Drug Abuse. 2011. "Commonly Abused Drugs Chart." National Institutes of Health. Accessed September 19. http://www.nida.nih.gov/DrugPages/DrugsofAbuse .html.

8

"Why Does Everyone Keep Telling Me to Relax?"— Mental and Emotional Health

Teens and Mental Illness

Children and adolescents struggle with the very same mental and emotional health issues that adults do, but these issues may be much harder to diagnose before the body and brain are fully developed. Some of the behaviors that many adults write off as "normal" adolescent behavior, or "normal" teenage rebellion, may actually be symptoms of larger psychiatric problems. Conversely, personality or energy changes that may simply be a natural part of a teen's development can erroneously be interpreted as signs of unstable mental health.

Mental disorders are so common in the United States that in any given year about a quarter of the adult population could be diagnosed with one or more disorders—and the average age of onset is just 14 (National Institute of Mental Health, 2011b). Despite this prevalence, mental illness is still highly stigmatized. The unemployment rate for Americans with serious mental illnesses is incredibly high at 90 percent (Mental Health America, 2007). Many people who suffer from mental illness have difficulty finding access to health insurance, because many disorders are considered "preexisting conditions" that exclude an individual from coverage. Yet those who require medication and therapy the most may not be able to afford them without insurance. Although the Americans with Disabilities Act of 1990 (amended in 2008) was written and enacted to protect all Americans with disabilities—including mental and emotional disorders—many adults and teens who struggle with mental illness still experience discrimination when trying to access housing, employment, and education (Americans with Disabilities Act, as Amended, 2008).

In order to fully support your teens' mental and emotional health and growth, it's important to have at least a basic understanding of some of the more common issues. Again, these aren't unique to adolescence, and may be more accurately diagnosed once a young person grows into adulthood, but many of the signs and symptoms begin to manifest in the adolescent years. You may already know that teens in your area or within a certain social group suffer more from an individual problem, but it's a good idea to familiarize yourself with all the issues that might affect your local teen population.

Anxiety Disorders

Anxiety, the most prominent symptom of anxiety disorders, is defined as "a mood characterized by apprehension and associated physical symptoms of tension (e.g., tense muscles, fast breathing, rapid heartbeat)" (Wienclaw and Davidson, 2009). The *Diagnostic and Statistical Manual of Mental Disorders*, or *DSM-IV*, recognizes the following anxiety disorders (American Psychiatric Association, 2000):

- **Panic disorder without agoraphobia**—recurring panic attacks, or attacks of intense fear or apprehension
- **Panic disorder with agoraphobia**—recurring panic attacks as well as avoidance of certain places or situations due to anxiety
- **Agoraphobia without history of panic disorder**—anxiety and panic around specific places or situations without actual panic attacks
- **Specific phobias**—anxiety related to a particular object (such as dogs, spiders, snakes) or situation (such as violent storms, driving at night, falling)
- **Social phobias**—fear of social situations or performance anxiety (such as public speaking or even eating in public)
- **Obsessive-compulsive disorder (OCD)**—afflicted individuals compelled to repeatedly perform some act (often a seemingly random one, such as touching a doorknob or washing their hands) to neutralize their anxiety
- **Post-traumatic stress disorder (PTSD)**—reliving a traumatic event long after the original trauma is over, with the same feelings of anxiety attached
- **Acute stress disorder**—similar to PTSD, but experienced immediately after the traumatic event
- **Generalized anxiety disorder**—six months or more of persistent, excessive worry and anxiety
- **Anxiety due to a general medical condition**—anxiety caused by some other medical condition
- **Substance-induced anxiety disorder**—anxiety caused by a drug or toxin

Generalized anxiety and panic disorders are more likely to develop in teens, while OCD and phobias often begin in childhood (Wienclaw and Davidson, 2009).

About 8 percent of teens (ages 13–18) have an anxiety disorder, with symptoms emerging when children are as young as six. Unfortunately, only about 18 percent of those teens—not even a quarter—receive mental health care (National Institute of Mental Health, 2011a). Some of this is certainly due to a lack of mental health awareness among the general public. Many parents and families don't have a history of seeking emotional or psychiatric help, so many family members may have suffered from undiagnosed mental health issues. Consequently, these adults have no framework of mental health care from which to support teens. Adults who were themselves told to "toughen up" or "shake it off" may have only the same advice to give to their children. As a result, teens may feel like failures if they are unable to "solve" their mental health problems on their own.

Symptoms of an anxiety disorder can include excessive worrying, paranoia, trouble sleeping, difficulty starting or finishing activities because of persistent worry, and anxiety or panic attacks. Panic attacks can be particularly alarming to a young person, as they are characterized by a sudden increase in heart rate and a shock of adrenaline. Many sufferers of panic attacks initially believe they are having a heart attack, and the speeding pulse and shakiness associated with an increase in adrenaline can often linger well after the initial attack. Sufferers may erroneously associate the attacks with whatever they were doing at the time and either avoid that activity, or regard it with such fear and trepidation that they can actually trigger another attack themselves.

Teens suffering from an anxiety disorder may have difficulty leaving the house or maintaining a normal activity level. They may also attempt to self-medicate in order to relax by using alcohol or someone else's prescription drugs, or exercising excessively. Those suffering from paranoia may be particularly disinclined to seek help, as they may question the motives of those around them and regard authority figures with suspicion.

Bipolar Disorder

Symptoms of bipolar disorder, once known as manic depression, include extreme mood swings, which can make the disorder very difficult to diagnose. Bipolar patients experiencing fatigue, depression, and listlessness can be diagnosed with depression, while those experiencing unusually high energy levels, pressured speech, and difficulty sleeping may be diagnosed with anxiety, psychosis, or even drug abuse. Indeed, over half of all bipolar patients have a history of substance abuse, and the emotional and physical extremes associated with cocaine use may mimic or mask bipolar symptoms (Ford-Martin, Odle, and Davidson, 2009a).

One large, nationally representative study suggests that at least half of all cases of bipolar disorder begin before age 25 (when the disorder is typically diagnosed). Children and teens with bipolar disorder can also have co-occurring disorders, such as attention deficit hyperactivity disorder (ADHD) or anxiety, which can either mask or exacerbate their bipolar symptoms (National Institute of Mental Health, 2012). While it is certainly controversial to diagnose children and adolescents with bipolar disorder, introducing the possibility to teens who are already seeking mental health help can cushion the blow of a later diagnosis. Along with schizophrenia and other forms of psychosis, bipolar disorder is frequently stereotyped in popular culture.

Teens may not know much about the disorder itself but may be well aware that it is often used as shorthand for "crazy."

Teens experiencing bipolar symptoms may believe they are experiencing a whole host of other problems—anxiety, paranoia, post-traumatic stress disorder, aggression—and may be treated accordingly by physicians or mental health professionals, but medication that treats only one or some bipolar symptoms may actually make matters worse. Some antidepressants, in particular, can stimulate manic episodes, while others may trigger what is known as *rapid cycling*—changing the mood from depressed to manic much more quickly (National Institute of Mental Health, 2012).

Depression

While just about everyone has experienced feelings of sadness and unhappiness, true depression is more than just feeling down in the dumps. Clinical depression is defined as "a psychiatric illness characterized by profound and persistent feelings of sadness, despair and/or worthlessness that interfere with daily functioning and personal relationships" (Ford-Martin, Odle, and Davidson, 2009b). About 11 percent of teens have a depressive disorder by age 18. Depression in teens, as in adults, is characterized by a loss of energy and interest in everyday activities, excessive sleeping or feelings of fatigue, lack of appetite, and social withdrawal. Depressive periods may be brief, lasting a few days or weeks, or, left untreated, may persist for years. There's still a lot we don't know about depression, including its true causes; scientists now believe imbalances in the brain's neurotransmitters are to blame, but the relative importance of serotonin, norepinephrine, and dopamine is still unclear (Ford-Martin, Odle, and Davidson, 2009b).

Teens are more likely to respond to treatment if it's given early, but there's a known risk of suicidal thinking and attempts when teens are given antidepressants (National Institute of Mental Health, 2011c). Since suicide is the third leading cause of death among adolescents (nearly 7 percent of high school students have attempted suicide), it's especially important for adults to monitor teens closely if they are prescribed antidepressants (American Academy of Pediatrics, 2011).

Again, teens showing signs of depression may be ignored by adults who write off their behavior as simply being "moody." Although it's true that many otherwise healthy teens may experience mood swings as their bodies and minds adjust to new hormones and the rapidly changing social sphere of adolescence, lethargy, flat affect, and a loss of interest in the activities and people a teen used to love are not "normal" teen behaviors.

ADHD

Attention-deficit hyperactivity disorder (commonly abbreviated as ADHD) is one of the most common childhood disorders, but it can persist into adolescence and adulthood.

Young people suffering from ADHD may have either mostly inattentive symptoms (lack of attention and focus, failure to listen or follow directions, slower reaction time), mostly hyperactive or impulsive symptoms (difficulty staying still, frequently moving or touching, impatience, speaking or acting without regard for the consequences), or a combination of both (U.S. Department of Health and Human Services, 2008).

Teens who suffer from ADHD may have been diagnosed as young children and have been taking medication ever since, or they may be trying to cope undiagnosed. Those who experience mostly symptoms of inattention may go undiagnosed for longer, as they may appear to be quiet, model students; their difficulty in focusing and following directions may go undiscovered, or be misinterpreted by adults as laziness. Adults may also primarily associate ADHD with hyperactivity—constant talking and motion—and not realize that symptoms may not always manifest in this "classic" way.

Teens with ADHD who aren't receiving adequate mental health support may believe they're stupid or lazy, since even their best efforts don't seem to result in good grades. They may also self-medicate; Ritalin and other ADHD medications are now common enough among young people that they may be used (and abused) recreationally.

Teens' Experience with Education and Mental Illness

Like teens with learning or developmental disabilities, teens with mental disorders often need more support in the classroom—but they don't always get it. Many teens who suffer from mental illness, particularly depression, may experience long absences from school that should be treated as medical issues, but are often seen as mere truancy, particularly if families and educators are equally in the dark about the true nature of the illness. Just as teens with ADHD may have difficulty concentrating in school and see their grades suffer as a result, teens with anxiety or other disorders may have difficulty simply *being* in school.

Mental health issues may manifest as a refusal to do work, reluctance to attend or participate in class, and other school-averse behaviors that often get teens labeled as troublemakers or burnouts. When these teens are given safe, individualized learning environments (which may mean out-of-district placement, or enrollment in unique programs within the building), they may thrive. Without that level of support, they are at risk of failing classes and dropping out entirely.

Signs to Watch For

All mental, emotional, and behavioral problems come with their own set of symptoms, but many overlap. You don't have to be able to *diagnose* a teen's problem (only a mental health professional should) to know that something isn't right. It's less important to memorize the facts and figures for each individual disorder than it is to pay attention to some bigger picture changes. Remember that you don't have to go it alone; if you've observed something in a teen that's worrying you but you don't feel confident enough to know whether it's a mental health issue, consider talking to a social worker, psychiatrist (specializing in teens), or other health care professional. You don't have to name names, but you may be more comfortable speaking to them before you have a teen in mind. That way you have a better idea of how the conversation might go should you need to call on them in an emergency situation.

Here are some common signs:

- **Extreme highs or lows.** Once you've gotten to know the teens in your library, you'll be used to the ones who may come in at any hour of the day singing at the top of their lungs or the ones who can spend hours silently curled up with a book. You'll know that high energy for one teen is just the baseline for another. What you should be on the lookout for are extreme *changes* in mood or energy level. Huge mood swings can be signs of something else, of course—like changes in diet, caffeine intake, or alcohol or drug abuse—but since these changes are manifesting themselves mentally and emotionally, it's a good idea to respond to them as you would any mental health issue.
- **Erratic behavior.** Many adults will tell you that teens *always* behave unpre-dictably—and to a certain extent, that's true. But a teen who's acting out of the ordinary (especially if they start giving away possessions or saying goodbye to close friends, which can be warning signs of suicidal thoughts), particularly one who doesn't recognize that they're acting strangely, is a teen to watch. Is your usually super-punctual afternoon volunteer showing up late or skipping days altogether? Is a teen who's usually no trouble at all in the library suddenly causing disruptions left and right? There might be something happening at home, or this could be a teen in crisis.
- **Changes in affect.** This one's a little tricky. It's easy to spot changes in *behavior*, but what about changes in *personality*? Some of this is about paying attention to mood, but it's also about watching teens' reactions. A teen who usually jumps right in to activities or socializing may hang back, but a personality change isn't just a matter of withdrawing from peers; a teen with a flat affect no longer seems to even *care* about his surroundings or what others are doing. It's also important not to just look for a flat or depressed affect; teens who seem unusually animated or who seem to be giving more weight to ordinarily inconsequential events or interactions may also be in trouble.
- **Increased risky behavior.** This is another area where symptoms of mental illness may overlap with symptoms of alcohol and drug abuse or other underly-ing issues. Look for teens who suddenly start being truant, who talk frankly

about sexual promiscuity, who boast of alcohol or drug use, or who start having confrontations with security or law enforcement. Many adults think *all* teens take risks. Research does actually suggest that adolescents are more motivated by pleasure-seeking than adults, in no small part due to the presence of dopamine in the brain. Dopamine is responsible for feelings of pleasure, and scientists have determined that there's more dopamine activity in the brain's reward center in adolescence than at any other life stage (Steinberg, 2011). But you know your teens: some of them are risk-takers, and some of them toe the line. The ones who suddenly show little regard for the consequences of their actions may very well be asking for help.

A Word about Confidentiality

While in many cases it's entirely appropriate (and in fact I've recommended it in this book) to discuss the lives and behaviors of your teens with other adults, mental health is a bit of a stickier subject. You may want to get a second opinion from a coworker if you're worried about a teen, but if you have *explicit knowledge* of a teen's mental or emotional health issues, it's not okay to share that with everyone unless you have that teen's consent.

In a school setting, the school nurse may share information about students with allergies or diabetes so that the whole staff can be prepared in case of an emergency, but she won't tell everyone about which students are taking medication or who's in therapy. Just as you wouldn't expect to know who's on an IEP (Individualized Education Plan) or receiving special education support if they weren't in your class, you shouldn't expect to know all the details about your teens' symptoms or treatment. If they confide in *you*, you have a responsibility to keep that information private—unless you think someone might be in danger.

If a teen tells you they're suicidal or that they're worried a friend might do something rash, yes, get emergency backup right away. If a teen tells you they don't want to keep taking medication or they think therapy isn't working, be very clear with that teen. Ask clear, respectful questions, and explain why you're asking: "Is it okay if I share this information with your mom/a teacher/your therapist? What you just told me worries me a little, and I want to make sure someone else who cares about you knows what's going on." Never promise teens that you'll keep a secret until you know what the secret is. (Swearing not to tell anyone about their latest crush is very, very different from swearing you won't tell anyone that they're "borrowing" lithium from a friend.)

Remember that you have no responsibility to share teens' circulation records or tell anyone else what they've been asking for or searching for on library computers, even if they've been checking out materials related to mental health issues or substance abuse. Just as you would defend your adult patrons' intellectual freedom and right to privacy, you should defend your teen patrons' rights as well. You may feel less comfortable refusing requests if they come from parents—especially if you work in a school setting, where teachers might reasonably be expected to act in loco parentis—but in these cases it's all the more important to have a policy in place stating that teens are responsible for their own behavior in the library and in the use of library materials. Teens who are curious about drugs aren't necessarily taking them, and teens who read about mental illness may not have experienced it firsthand. Your teen patrons need the freedom to explore all kinds of information—even information about controversial subjects—without fear that the adults in their lives are looking over their shoulders at the circulation logs.

Ways to Get Involved without Getting Involved

Not every teen who has mental health concerns or needs is going to feel comfortable coming to you directly, and *you're* not always going to feel confident enough to get involved. None of this means that you can't offer resources to all teens in your library, whether you ever have a conversation with them or not. Information and solutions that don't *appear* to come from you personally can also allow a teen to approach these conversations at their own pace, having a face-to-face discussion when they're comfortable rather than feeling like an adult is intruding in their business.

Partner with a Social Worker or Counselor

By "partner" I don't necessarily mean *literally* partner; I'm not suggesting you train a clinical social worker to catalog graphic novels or plant a counselor in the corner of the teen room. That would be weird, and it wouldn't work very well, and you would quickly develop a reputation as *that creepy librarian who's always asking how that makes me feel*. Instead, I mean have an informal (or formal, if you're lucky enough to get a social worker on the library payroll) relationship with someone who supports teens' emotional and mental well-being for a living.

When teens come to you looking for help, or when teens you care about aren't acting like themselves, wouldn't it be nice if you had a local professional to consult with, who could give you suggestions and even take referrals if teens ask you directly for help finding mental health support? Establishing a relationship with a clinician, therapist, or other social worker also helps the mental health community in your area learn more about the most pressing local youth issues. Teens who are forced to see a psychiatrist or social worker may respond with anger or silence; they're not inclined to open up to a complete stranger. Getting a referral from an adult they already know and trust (that's you), however, can make a teen feel more comfortable with a new face, and more willing to be honest about what's really happening.

Offer Resources Online

It's never a bad idea to have information readily available on your library website. You should offer teens both contact information for local mental health clinics and providers (particularly those who take teen patients) as well as easy access to all the facts and figures they might want to research about a given issue or disorder. You'll know the community organizations closest to you, but here are a few national resources to get you started:

- **Cope Care Deal** (http://www.copecaredeal.org/)
  A product of the Annenberg Foundation Trust at Sunnylands, Cope Care Deal offers teens information and strategies for living with mental illness.
- **National Suicide Prevention Lifeline** (http://www.suicidepreventionlifeline.org/)
  Along with the hotline (1-800-273-TALK), this website gives visitors of all ages a chance to find local crisis centers, learn more about the warning signs of suicide, and get help or get involved.
- **Mental Health America** (http://www.mentalhealthamerica.net/)
  MHA offers facts and statistics on a wide range of mental health issues, including sections dedicated specifically to teens and families.
- **National Institute of Mental Health** (http://www.nimh.nih.gov/)
  NIMH provides detailed information on all mental disorders, broken down by topic, age, or gender. There's also a section for those who may be in search of more immediate help, which includes both general information (such as overviews of medication) and emergency solutions.

Keep Your Resources Current

As with all resources related to the sciences, it's especially crucial to make sure all your materials dealing with mental health are current and geared toward teens. Teens may seek out more advanced titles if they're just researching a disorder for a school project, but teens who are experiencing mental illness (or are concerned they might be) need materials that are straightforward and digestible. Teens can be easily turned off by dated covers and illustrations, so check your mental health section often to make sure you haven't left any acid-washed jeans behind.

It's also important to keep your materials up-to-date because psychiatric services for youth are evolving every day. It wasn't that long ago that scientists and doctors assumed adult psychiatric medicines would be perfectly safe for teens; today we know that many children and teens need much lower doses of medications, and that some medications should be closely monitored because teen side effects can be extreme.

Think about Your Space

If you had any input on the aesthetics and configuration of your teen space, you probably tried to make it inviting and exciting—but how would a teen suffering from anxiety or ADHD be able to interact with the space? Sensory stimuli that you might never notice, like the ambient noise of computers or the way light filters into a room when a door is opened, may actually be a huge distraction (or frightening trigger) to some teens. If teens tell you that something about the room bothers them, don't dismiss those concerns; they may not even be able to put their finger on *what* is so unsettling, but it's important that these teens feel heard and welcome.

Keep Resources Visible and Discreet

As with information about sexual health and abuse, information on mental health can intimidate or embarrass teens. They may not want to ask you directly for these resources, or they may not want to risk their friends and peers seeing them looking for that kind of information. Make sure you offer plenty of passive, disposable resources—brochures in multiple locations, magnets or stickers with pertinent hotline and clinic information, and business cards from local social workers and therapists. You may also want to consider keeping a shelf of resources that circulate informally; let teens know that they can use them in the library or take them home, and they won't have to walk up to you at the desk.

You Don't Have to Overshare

Teens often feel like all the adults in their lives know their business. I know that when I was first diagnosed with depression as a teenager, it seemed like every teacher at my high school suddenly wanted to talk about it. They all told me it was nothing to be ashamed of, and several even admitted that *they'd* had mental health struggles or were on medication. While I admire their candor, at the time I was deeply uncomfortable with these revelations. I didn't want to know these things about adults who weren't particularly close to me.

While it's certainly your choice whether or not to disclose your mental health status to teens—just as it's your choice whether to tell *anyone* in your life, from coworkers to potential partners—you should feel absolutely no obligation to share this element of your personal life with teens. While some of them may appreciate knowing that adults (especially adults they like) survived their teenage years and have coped with mental illness, others may see you as intruding into their lives. Many teens won't have fully formed views about mental and emotional health, and may treat you differently as a result. Others may feel like you're trying to diagnose them, and they may not be comfortable with their own diagnosis yet—or you may have them pegged all wrong.

References

American Academy of Pediatrics. 2011. "Critical Adolescent Health Issues—Mental Health and Substance Abuse." American Academy of Pediatrics. Accessed September 16. http://www.aap.org/sections/adolescenthealth/mentalhealth.cfm.

American Psychiatric Association. 2000. *Diagnostic and Statistical Manual of Mental Disorders* (4th ed., text rev.). Washington, DC: American Psychiatric Association.

Americans with Disabilities Act of 1990, as Amended. 2008. United States Code (P.L. 101–336, July 26, 1990). http://www.ada.gov/pubs/adastatute08.htm#subchapterI.

Ford-Martin, Paula Anne, Teresa G. Odle, and Tish Davidson. 2009a. "Bipolar Disorder." In *The Gale Encyclopedia of Medicine*, edited by Jacqueline L. Longe. Detroit: Gale. Accessed via online subscription.

———. 2009b. "Depression." In *The Gale Encyclopedia of Medicine*, edited by Jacqueline L. Longe. Detroit: Gale. Accessed via online subscription.

Mental Health America. 2007. "Position Statement 31: Employment Development of Services for Adults in Recovery for Mental Illness." Mental Health America. June 10. http://www.nmha.org/go/position-statements/31.

National Institute of Mental Health. 2011a. "Anxiety Disorders in Children and Adolescents (Fact Sheet)." National Institutes of Health. Last reviewed April 29. http://nimh.nih.gov/health/publications/anxiety-disorders-in-children-and-adolescents/index.shtml.

———. 2011b. "Any Disorder among Adults." National Institutes of Health. Accessed September 20. http://nimh.nih.gov/statistics/1ANYDIS_ADULT.shtml.

———. 2011c. "Depression in Children and Adolescents (Fact Sheet)." National Institutes of Health. Last reviewed April 25. http://nimh.nih.gov/health/publications/depression-in-children-and-adolescents/index.shtml.

———. 2012. "Bipolar Disorder in Children and Adolescents (Fact Sheet)." National Institutes of Health. Last reviewed February 13. http://nimh.nih.gov/health/publications/bipolar-disorder-in-children-and-adolescents/index.shtml.

Steinberg, Laurence. 2011. "Demystifying the Adolescent Brain." *Educational Leadership* 68, no. 7: 42–46.

U.S. Department of Health and Human Services. 2008. "Attention Deficit Hyperactivity Disorder (ADHD)." http://nimh.nih.gov/health/publications/attention-deficit-hyperactivity-disorder/complete-index.shtml.

Wienclaw, Ruth A., and Davidson, Tish. 2009. "Anxiety Disorders." In *The Gale Encyclopedia of Medicine*, 3rd ed., edited by Jacqueline L. Longe. Detroit: Gale. Accessed via online subscription.

9

"You Wanna Fight about It?"— Teen Violence and Juvenile Justice

Youth Crime

There were 2.11 million juvenile arrests in 2008 alone. Of the delinquency cases tried in juvenile court that year, probation was ordered in 50 percent of them. Like adults on probation, youth on probation must meet with a probation officer regularly. They may also be ordered to perform community service, pay restitution for their crimes, or undergo drug treatment or counseling—all as conditions of their probation, intended to keep youth from incarceration (Office of Juvenile Justice and Delinquency Prevention, 2010). A new study of more than a decade of Bureau of Labor statistics suggests that nearly one in three people will be arrested by the time they are 23 (Brame et al., 2012)—meaning experience with the juvenile justice system (or its adult counterpart) may be much more common than we once thought.

Theft is by far the most common crime reported at schools, but most school day crimes (crimes committed on a day when school is in session) by juveniles take place in the hours immediately following school—meaning efforts to curb after-school violence should be more successful than youth curfews (laws prohibiting minors from being on the streets after a certain hour) (Brame et al., 2012).

Known juvenile offenders were involved in at least 908 murders in the United States in 2008—9 percent of all murders. All states have provisions to try juveniles as adults, although many also extend juvenile court authority after an offender has turned 18. At least 22 states and the District of Columbia have no minimum age at which a juvenile may be sentenced as an adult. (Sixteen other states set the minimum age at 14.) In 2008, young women accounted for 17 percent of the juvenile violent crime arrests, 36 percent of the juvenile property crime arrests, and 33 percent of the juvenile disorderly conduct arrests, while youth under the age of 15 accounted for 27 percent of the juvenile violent crime arrests and 29 percent of the juvenile property crime arrests (Brame et al., 2012).

In 2007, there were fewer than 87,000 juveniles in residential placement (incarcerated); 14 percent of these were female. More than 23,000 were 17-year-olds, more than any other single age group (Brame et al., 2012). Nearly 10 percent of incarcerated youth are held in adult facilities. These teens are five times more likely to be sexually assaulted and eight times more likely to commit suicide than youth in juvenile facilities (Coalition for Juvenile Justice, 2011b). Some 50 to 75 percent of incarcerated youth have diagnosable mental health problems. In fact, two-thirds of juvenile detention centers hold youth who are just waiting for mental health treatment; in 33 states, youth with mental illness can be held in juvenile facilities without any charges against them (Coalition for Juvenile Justice, 2011d). Youth with emotional disabilities or who are suffering from mental health issues are more than three times more likely than their peers to be arrested before finishing school. In Pennsylvania, for example, students with disabilities make up 13 percent of the school-age population, but 24 percent of the population of youth referred to the police or juvenile justice (Coalition for Juvenile Justice, 2011c).

Black youth are also seriously overrepresented in the juvenile justice system. Black students are more likely than their white peers to be suspended, expelled, or arrested for similar conduct while at school. In one particularly extreme example, in 2003 blacks made up 50 percent of all Chicago Public Schools (CPS) students, yet they made up more than 77 percent of all arrests in CPS (Coalition for Juvenile Justice, 2011c).

Youth as Victims

Between 1980 and 2008, more than five thousand juveniles were murdered, making up over 10 percent of all murders in 2008. That year juvenile victims were 30 percent female, 47 percent black, and half were killed by a firearm. In 2007, homicide was the fourth leading cause of death for those ages 1 to 11. It was the second leading cause of death for youth 12 to 17. Youth are more likely to be the victims of crime between the hours of three and four on school days than on nonschool days (Office of Juvenile Justice and Delinquency Prevention, 2010).

Most young homicide victims between 1980 and 2008 were killed by a family member (usually a parent), while family members were rarely involved in the killing of juveniles ages 15 through 17. A full quarter of juvenile murder victims ages 15 through 17 were killed by a stranger. Female victims were much more likely than male victims to have been killed by a family member (Office of Juvenile Justice and Delinquency Prevention, 2010).

For every ten white homicide victims ages 7 to 17 between 1990 and 2007, there were 25 suicide victims—a ratio of 10 to 25. The corresponding ratio was 10 to 1 for black youth and 10 to 4 for Hispanic youth. The suicide rate for Native American youth was more than double the white (non-Hispanic) rate and triple the rates for other ethnic groups (Office of Juvenile Justice and Delinquency Prevention, 2010). It should also be noted that there are more than four times the number of youth suicides in correctional facilities than in the general population of youths (Coalition for Juvenile Justice, 2011d).

Juvenile offenders are much more likely than adult offenders to choose sexual assault targets under the age of 18 (95 percent of juvenile sexual assault victims are under 18, compared with 64 percent of adult offenders) (Office of Juvenile Justice and Delinquency Prevention, 2010).

Gangs

According to the "National Survey of American Attitudes on Substance Abuse XV: Teens and Parents" (National Center on Addiction and Substance Abuse at Columbia University, 2010), 45 percent of high school students report that there are gangs or self-reported gang members in their school. Thirty-five percent of middle school students answered the same question in the affirmative. There's a stark difference between reporting in public versus private schools, however; 46 percent of public school students reported gangs and gang members at their school, while only 2 percent of private school students did the same. Some of the most dangerous gang activities may actually take place in and around schools, where gang members run into each other (or seek each other out) in common areas, or even attend school largely to conduct gang activities (Arciaga, Sakamoto, and Jones, 2010).

There's also evidence that schools are largely in the dark—or in denial—about gang members and gang activities within their walls. More than one-third of principals (36 percent) reported gang activity in their immediate community surroundings, yet only 5 percent reported gangs in their own schools. Some of this denial is certainly intentional; administrators may feel that admitting gang activity is admitting disciplinary defeat, or they may fear violating their own confidentiality regulations by revealing names of students to the police or the media. It's also true, however, that many teachers and administrators aren't trained to recognize gang activity, or don't feel qualified (or even physically capable) to stop it. Some may even make gang conflicts worse, by playing favorites, keeping rival gang members in the same room while they await punishment after an altercation, or making fun of or insulting gang members (Arciaga, Sakamoto, and Jones, 2010).

Teachers—and librarians—should be trained specifically in gang violence prevention in order to recognize the colors and symbols of gangs in their community and help stop confrontations before they start, but here are several warning signs that may indicate building gang tension or impending gang violence:

- **Confrontational eye contact.** Look for teens who appear to be staring each other down or trying to provoke a confrontation nonverbally. Two teens who are locked in a staring contest may also pull the attention of other teens around them, who sense the tension in the room.

- **Hand signs.** Gang signs usually consist of alphabet letters or symbols made with the hands. Gang members may show these symbols to fellow gang members, or they may flash them at a rival gang as a provocation. These signs may not follow standard ASL or other sign language/alphabet rules.
- **Verbal challenges.** Members may shout out the name of their own gang—which may very well make little sense to you if you're not familiar with the names of area gangs—or attempt to challenge a rival gang. These challenges may sound like simple teenage posturing, but coming from a gang member they should always be taken as a legitimate threat of violence.
- **Group confrontations.** You may think you're only seeing a group of teens standing around talking to one another, but pay close attention to the teens involved. Several members of one gang may "square off" against another physically before a fight.
- **Gang colors.** Most gangs adopt a color or colors to signify their group, and may take the display of rival colors as a direct threat. These go beyond the stereotypical Crip and Blood signifiers (although those, too, should be taken seriously). It can be particularly tricky if a gang adopts the same colors as a school's or sports team's official colors, which may unwittingly be worn by non–gang members.
- **Showing weapons.** Gangs may drive by an area—including your school or library—with weapons visible as a warning to rival gangs. They may also flash weapons, including guns or knives stashed in pockets or waistbands, to prove their threats are serious.
- **Advance warning.** Teens who learn about an impending gang conflict or violence, whether they're gang members themselves or not, may try to report their concerns anonymously; they may leave unsigned notes in public places or call with a warning and hang up before identifying themselves in any way. These threats should always be taken seriously, whether or not you have a reliable identification for their source; teens who give you these kinds of warnings may be risking their own lives to do so.

Prevention

Taxpayers save an estimated two million dollars for each youth prevented from entering a life of crime (Coalition for Juvenile Justice, 2011e). Yet since the 2002 fiscal year, federal funding for preventing or reducing juvenile delinquency has decreased by 50 percent, while federal funding of policing, prosecution, and incarceration has risen by 60 percent (Coalition for Juvenile Justice, 2011a). Intensive probation decreases the rate of youth offense at a mere one-third the cost of incarceration (Coalition for Juvenile Justice, 2011e).

In order to prevent juvenile crimes, teens need a combination of proactive factors:

- **Protective family.** Teens who are the most successful at completing probation or avoiding juvenile justice altogether are those with invested, involved family members who are able to stay engaged with their child's school, extracurricular activities, and general well-being. Protective family members show up at all juvenile and criminal court proceedings, testify on behalf of their children, and ensure positive community engagement when their children are able to avoid incarceration. These families do more than show up, however; they genuinely love and care for their children.
- **Positive personal attributes.** Teens who successfully avoid or navigate the juvenile justice system do so by developing positive personal attributes. These may include intelligence, determination, resilience, and loyalty—as well as social skills, such as the ability to problem-solve in order to find alternatives to violence.
- **Safe schools.** Youth can't succeed without safe and positive schools that set high standards. Teens who are worried about being assaulted or robbed at school are less likely to be able to concentrate on their studies.
- **Solid communities.** Communities that offer youth opportunities—job and volunteer opportunities, as well as teams and organizations to be a part of—are communities that invest in youth and offer a level of social control that teens need.
- **Peer groups.** Teens need peer engagement to succeed. They need friends, but they also need all levels of acquaintances. They need the opportunity to experience socializing with their peers, including those they may not particularly like, in order to develop social skills and coping mechanisms.
- **Engaged adults.** Beyond involved families, teens also need other adult role models to be involved in their lives and supervise youth activities. They need committed teachers, coaches, tutors, mentors, and employers (Coalition for Juvenile Justice, 2011e).

If these necessary ingredients for teen success sound awfully familiar, they should; many of these requirements for a safe and productive youth overlap with the Developmental Assets covered way back in Chapter 2. The requirements for a successful teen *in general* are the same for a teen who avoids involvement in the juvenile or criminal justice system, and the obstacles that may stand in the way for your average teen will put up serious roadblocks for a teen already at risk of turning to delinquency or crime.

All Teens Suffer from Youth Crime

If you work with inner-city youth, there's a very good chance that all or nearly all the teens who use your library have been touched by crime or violence in some way. They will be used to lockdown drills and tight security at their schools, including metal detectors, armed school police officers or security guards, and random (or not-so-random) searches of lockers and backpacks. Some may have friends or family members who are involved with local gangs, or they may have been approached themselves for membership. Too many know someone—possibly even a loved one—who has been the victim of violence, including murder.

If you *don't* work in a major metropolitan area, however, it would still be a mistake to assume none of your teens are affected by violence, gangs, or youth crime in general. Rural and suburban gangs *do* exist, and teens in these areas may live under the threat of violence. Perhaps more pertinent to *your* day-to-day work with young adults, teens everywhere are impacted by the delinquent or criminal acts of teens—whether real, or merely perceived.

Profiling Teens

Whether it's the shop owner who follows teens around a store to make sure they don't steal anything or the police officer who sees a group of teens and immediately asks them to separate, many adults respond negatively to teens based solely on age. Teens may be unfairly watched, accused of littering or vandalism they didn't commit simply because they're in the area, or kicked out of public (or private) areas either entirely because of their age, or due to behaviors that would be tolerated if the "perpetrators" were adults.

It's important here to note that teens of color are often targeted more for this kind of profiling than white teens. While white teens certainly still may suffer from age-based prejudice, black and Latino teens are more likely to have similar actions labeled rowdy or disruptive when they are in stores or awaiting public transportation, just as they are more likely to be punished in schools for behavior that their white teens may carry out with impunity.

Youth Curfews

A common response (or reaction) to youth delinquency or crime is the imposition of curfews for youth. Under these local or state laws, youth under a certain age (often 18, but sometimes 16) cannot lawfully be out on the streets after a specified evening hour without an accompanying adult. Police may especially patrol skate parks, arcades, outdoor malls or shopping centers, or school buildings, assumed to be the most likely hangouts for unaccompanied minors. The general argument is that teens—especially groups of teens—without adult supervision after dark are more likely to cause trouble, so why not nip that trouble in the bud?

As we discussed when looking at teen crime rates, however, most teen delinquency and crime takes place in the hours immediately following the school day—*not* after dark. Prevention programs that focus on a stretch of time when teens are statistically *unlikely to commit crimes*, then, aren't likely to decrease the overall teen crime rate.

Instead, they're likely to waste resources on officers patrolling the neighborhood for errant teens, not to mention further alienate many teens (who like to "congregate" at night without adult supervision, but honestly aren't doing anything wrong) from adults and law enforcement in particular.

You may think youth curfew laws have little to do with your library. After all, if you work in a school library, you aren't likely to be open when curfews take effect, and if you work in a public library that's open after dark, well, you're a supervising adult, right? Problem solved! . . . except that teens still have to worry about getting from the library to home. Even states that don't have curfew laws may regulate teen night driving, leaving teens in a bind when they want to get from point A to point B. Teens who violate curfew laws may have many of their privileges revoked, including their ability to visit the library alone or stay in the library after school.

Coping Mechanisms

Teens who have experienced violence, or who live with the threat of violence as part of daily life, have to adapt to survive. They assess their environment differently, speak differently, and act differently from teens whose everyday lives *don't* include the threat of violence. Some of these coping mechanisms may be invisible to an adult whose own life isn't marked in such a way, but others may actually lead adults to suspect a teen of being involved in gangs or violence—when really they've just adopted language and mannerisms to help them cope with daily threats of violence.

These coping mechanisms may include talking the way other peers talk (posturing about toughness, even verbal threats or reactions to threats), adopting tough or macho physical postures (never letting someone enter your personal space unanswered, taking up a lot of space wherever you go, keeping a strategic vantage point in any room so that you can see oncoming threats as well as potential exits), and adopting certain tough attitudes. These attitudes may include feigning a lack of interest in schoolwork (to avoid being labeled an egghead or a wuss), reacting to threats with threats (to avoid being perceived as weak), and distancing oneself from "weaker" peers or adults (to avoid any suspicion of snitching to authority figures).

It's important for you to realize that not all the teens who come into your library talking or acting hard are thugs. Some of them would probably love to be more involved with library programs, but they've developed an image that doesn't involve a passion for books or academics. It may be harder for you to gain the trust of these teens, but if you keep responding to their loud, aggressive behaviors with escalating threats of losing library privileges or getting kicked out of the building, you very likely will never get to know the thoughtful teens underneath that hard exterior. These aren't merely teens who are trying to gain acceptance from their peers or put on a macho act; these are teens who have seen friends and loved ones shot, stabbed, or violently beaten right in front of them. The tough "act" is a very necessary survival skill.

Escalation

Of course, when you combine teens who may actually be at risk of committing crimes or violent acts, teens who are putting on a tough exterior in order to survive, and adults—many of whom may not have grown up in the community in which they now work, meaning they may understand very little of the social dynamics at play—you run the risk of even minor confrontations escalating, and quickly.

Teens who are protecting their reputation, whether they're truly on their way to a life of crime or just adopting the language and behaviors of their peers, may feel that they can't give ground to any potential rival—even an adult. They view any reprimand from authority (from a polite request to remove a hat or hood to a police officer making inquiries) as a potential threat, an opportunity for someone else to get the upper hand in front of their rivals. Saving face is of the utmost importance. This can lead teens—even teens who have *absolutely nothing to hide* and who *know* they've done nothing wrong—to refuse to follow a request or order, to stand their ground when complying with a request would be easy, and to turn a simple question into a yelling match. These teens are likely to be labeled troublemakers, quickly gain a bad reputation with teachers and adults, and get into physical as well as verbal altercations.

Teens in the Justice System Suffer

Whether rightly or wrongly accused of crimes, teens who try to lead normal lives after being a part of the juvenile or criminal justice system (both on probation or in confinement) find many new obstacles in their path when they return to life with their peers.

Gaps in Education

Although all youth in confinement should have access to education, the value of that education may vary greatly from one facility to the next. Teens who were once enrolled in public schools may find themselves in "classrooms" with an emphasis on vocational skills or the GED, which, while certainly valuable for many teens (and adults), are not every teen's dream of education. Teens who are in and out of juvenile detention and other facilities may find it hard to reenter their schools and classrooms (indeed, arrest may be grounds for exclusion for many schools), and even if they can reenroll they are often forced to repeat classes or whole years in order to maintain enough credits to hope to graduate.

Teens who are forced to enroll in new schools or districts because of their history with the justice system may run up against many of the same obstacles that homeless youth face: a lack of consistency from school to school, difficulty engaging with a school community when they know they may be uprooted again, and difficulty keeping up with materials for school if their parents have already paid for textbooks in one school that aren't used in another.

It's also important to note that even students who haven't made it so far as criminal arrest or juvenile confinement may still have very disrupted educational experiences. Frequent school suspensions, particularly coupled with teachers who offer little flexibility on test and project dates, leave many teens woefully behind in all subjects. Even a single suspension, if poorly timed, can put a teen far behind his peers and at greater risk of failing or dropping out.

Employment Difficulties

Teens who have ever been arrested, put on probation or in confinement, and even those who have been suspended or expelled may have serious trouble finding gainful employment. Many (if not most) employers will ask about an applicant's criminal history, and although juvenile records are often sealed once a teen reaches 18 (unless he or she did not comply with the terms of probation), those records are very much open when the applicant is still a minor. Employers are generally wary of hiring adult convicts and show the same suspicion when considering hiring juvenile delinquents.

For teens on probation, although holding down a steady job would foster many of the positive attributes so vital to a teen's recovery and success, the hours of many jobs conflict too much with strict terms of probation (checking in with a probation officer, performing a certain number of community service hours, and adhering to set curfews). It's true that many probation officers are able to set teens up with part-time work that accommodates these terms, but teens who strike out on their own for work are often stymied.

Treated Like a Criminal

Even beyond employers, many adults simply won't give a teen with a delinquent or criminal past a fair shake. Prejudice from adults can lead teens on probation or release to withdraw from adults or even their peers. It can also keep them from engaging with groups or activities that might greatly help their chances of developing positive values or reintegrating with their peers.

For teens without a supportive family life, the worst prejudice may be suffered at home. A teen returning on probation or from confinement may see all trust dissolved, privileges revoked indefinitely, and nothing but grief from parents and family members. The guilt and scorn parents may heap on a teen can be particularly caustic if another family member (say, an absent parent) also has a history within the justice system; now the errant teen is "just like" Mom or Uncle Frank, even if the teen's infraction was clearly nowhere near the scale of the adult crime.

Making Your Library Safe for Everyone

Whatever the climate is in your neighborhood, whether you're meeting your first teen on probation or welcoming back several who have been in confinement before, you need tools to make sure all of your teens can get along with one another (and adults) in your library—and to make sure all teens have equal access to employment, education, and all library resources.

- **Offer gang training for everyone.** Make sure everyone in the library—including any security guards or school police officers—have appropriate gang training. Contact your local law enforcement or specific gang prevention organizations in order to tailor this training to your community and your library. Anyone working in the library should have a basic familiarity with local gang names, colors, and symbols. You should also have clear policies in place outlining your ban on weapons, gang colors, and gang activity.
- **Normalize your security.** Do your security guards just pace back and forth, or read the newspaper until there's a bag to be searched? Have your teen patrons ever seen your security staff interacting with patrons (both teen and adult) in a pleasant, ordinary way, or are they only known for intervening in emergency situations? You may not be in a position to dictate what your security staff members do and don't do while they're at the library, but you're certainly in a position to at least integrate these employees *socially*. Invite them to lunch or to join an activity in the teen area. Even asking for help with some heavy lifting can help teens see that security guards are people (and vice versa).
- **Provide de-escalation training.** Beyond gang training, you and your staff should also be well versed in general de-escalation techniques. These are ways to keep small confrontations—whether between teens, or between teens and adults—from exploding into violent or dangerous situations. If you work in a school, there's a good chance your district employs someone who delivers restraint and de-escalation training (this is often someone who works particularly with special education populations), or that your district would arrange for professional development specifically in this area.
- **Partner with mediation groups.** Find out what kind of juvenile justice organizations in your community offer either direct mediation services, or training for adults and youth on mediation techniques. Often teens in conflict (particularly those in gangs) who are interrupted by adults fake reconciliation until they can be alone to continue (or escalate) the fight; these same teens may react very differently when approached instead by peers who offer mediation.
- **Help teens in confinement.** If you take duplicate copies out of circulation or don't need (quality) donations that come from the community, consider making a donation to your local youth detention facilities. Jails and detention

centers in general are usually sorely lacking when it comes to books and other educational resources, so a donation of even a few books could go a long way. You might also consider loaning out a set of resources to set up a mobile library for teens in confinement. Some facilities may even let you sign in as a visitor to give book talks or take requests.

- **Connect with employers.** Teens looking for work may use the local library simply to check the help-wanted ads, but you can go one further by contacting employers or staffing organizations who understand the unique needs of youth with a juvenile justice history. You may even be able to set up workshops at the library to focus on filling out an application, creating a résumé, and making employment work with school or probation.
- **Offer educational access.** There's a good chance your library collection already includes test prep materials for the SAT, PSAT, and ACT; why not include GED test prep and access to alternative school programs? Try to make your computer access rules flexible for teens who may need to enroll in online courses or complete test prep materials online. Consider partnering with local high schools (including alternative schools and school-within-a-school programs) to offer course content online and jointly offer college and vocational fairs or workshops.
- **Expand your focus.** Cross-shelving (whether adult to teen or teen to younger children) in public libraries is often hotly debated, but consider offering titles at a lower reading level (including hi-lo titles, which offer teen subject matter at a considerably lower reading difficulty) as part of your teen collection. Teens with gaps in formal education may suffer greatly when it comes to reading, but they might be too proud to enter the children's room to find appropriate books.

References

Arciaga, Michelle, Wayne Sakamoto, and Errika Fearbry Jones. 2010. "Responding to Gangs in the School Setting." National Gang Center. http://www.nationalgangcenter.gov/Content/Documents/Bulletin-5.pdf.

Brame, Robert, Michael C. Turner, Raymond Paternoster, and Shawn D. Bushway. 2012. "Cumulative Prevalence of Arrest from Ages 8 to 23 in a National Sample." *Pediatrics* 129, no. 1: 21–28.

Coalition for Juvenile Justice. 2011a. "2011 Federal Funding Fact Sheet." Coalition for Juvenile Justice. Accessed September 21. http://www.juvjustice.org/media/factsheets/factsheet_15.pdf.

———. 2011b. "Conditions of Confinement for Young Offenders." Coalition for Juvenile Justice. Accessed September 21. http://www.juvjustice.org/media/factsheets/factsheet_4.pdf.

———. 2011c. "Ensuring School Engagement and Success vs. Exclusion for Youth at Risk of Delinquency." Accessed September 21. http://www.juvjustice.org/media/factsheets/factsheet_11.pdf.

————. 2011d. "Mental Health Needs of Youth and Young Offenders." Coalition for Juvenile Justice. Accessed September 21. http://www.juvjustice.org/media/factsheets/factsheet_8.pdf.

————. 2011e. "Prevention: Saving Lives and Dollars." Coalition for Juvenile Justice. Accessed September 21. http://www.juvjustice.org/media/factsheets/factsheet_9.pdf.

National Center on Addiction and Substance Abuse at Columbia University. 2010. "National Survey of American Attitudes on Substance Abuse XV: Teens and Parents." Columbia University. http://www.casacolumbia.org/upload/2010/20100819teensurvey.pdf.

Office of Juvenile Justice and Delinquency Prevention. 2010. "Statistical Briefing Book." U.S. Department of Justice, Office of Justice Programs. http://www.ojjdp.gov/ojstatbb/default.asp.

10

"Did You See What She Wrote on My Wall?"—Teens and Technology

The Technology

The technological world facing teens today is fundamentally different from that of twenty, ten, or even five years ago. Cell phones, once cumbersome and used primarily by a narrow section of the business world, now rest in the pockets and purses of every-one from elementary school students to retirees. The days of interminable downloads on dial-up modems are gone, replaced by high-speed mobile networks and free Wi-Fi in every McDonald's. MP3s and portable media players have turned the music industry on its ear, while e-books and e-readers continue to impact the publishing world (not to mention the library world). Even those of us who grew up on Star Trek couldn't have predicted the still-rising prevalence of touch screens and tablets in our daily lives.

Much has been made of the differences between so-called "digital natives"—those who are growing up in an increasingly media-saturated environment, with every imaginable technology at their fingertips—and "digital immigrants," who must adapt to the same technological environment as newcomers, born into very different worlds. It may not be particularly helpful to draw this divide strictly on generational lines, because many of us born before the Millennials are every bit as technologically adept. Nevertheless, it is important to recognize that while our *skills* may match those of the teens we serve (and, indeed, may even surpass them), our *experiences* are still very much unique. We watched technology in every arena evolve—in many cases within a matter of years—and render older methods obsolete, but most teens now lack the collective memory of that progression. They enter a world where the latest and greatest is simply par for the course.

With a backdrop of all these shiny toys, however, many aspects of teen life remain fundamentally unchanged. Just as they have for decades, teens find themselves in the midst of sometimes overwhelming physical and emotional changes. Well-established friendships from childhood give way to new social circles, and new romantic entangle-ments. Teens tease, test, and question one another—and the adults in their lives.

They learn from their mistakes, and repeat them. They fall in and out of love and like, practicing kindness and cruelty while they learn they are capable of each. Make no mistake: teens were bullies long before they could be cyberbullies, and they sent each other racy notes (yes, even racy pictures) when pen and paper were the only game in town. New technologies may change the ways these behaviors play out (and make for more sensational, not to mention immediate, stories on the evening news), but technology does not *create* these behaviors.

This chapter focuses on the technologies that are the most relevant to today's teens, with an emphasis on how use of these technologies (both inside and outside your library) can impact your work with teens, as well as ways technology use intersects with the topics already discussed in the previous chapters. The impact of emerging technology use on any of the aforementioned topics may be as straightforward as a teen researching sensitive topics from the privacy of a home computer or as complex as an abuser using cell phone minutes to control a victim. In some cases technology may simply be a vehicle for discussion or inquiry, while in others it may be a catalyst.

Cell Phones

Some 75 percent of all teens now own cell phones, up from just 45 percent in 2004 (Lenhart et al., 2010). For context, 82 percent of adults own cell phones, a number that has risen since 2004 but remained relatively steady since 2009 (Lenhart, 2010). Seventy-two percent of teens (or 88 percent of teen cell phone users) send text messages, an impressive increase from 51 percent in 2006 (Lenhart et al., 2010). Additionally, more than half of teens text daily—meaning the frequency of texting has overtaken *every other form of communication* for teens, including face-to-face conversation (Lenhart et al., 2010).

That statistic might not seem so significant if we saw similar patterns among adult cell phone users. And adults certainly do text; the number of adults sending and receiving texts jumped from 65 percent to 72 percent in just six months (Lenhart, 2010), which would seem to put adults and teens on equal footing when it comes to texting. But this number alone doesn't take into account the *volume* of texts sent and received. Adult texters generally send and receive a median of ten texts a day, while teen texters send and receive a median of 50. That means teens ages 12 to 17 send and receive (on average) *five times* more texts per day than their adult counterparts (Lenhart, 2010). One in three teens sends upwards of 100 texts a day, while half send 50 or more (Lenhart et al., 2010).

This isn't to say that teens use their phones *exclusively* for texting, although they certainly text more than they use any other phone function. Voice calling is still a well-used feature—especially when it comes to communicating with parents. Sixty-eight percent of teens with cell phones say they talk to their parents at least once a day (Lenhart et al., 2010). Interestingly, while 20 percent say they don't text their parents, only 4 percent say they never *call* parents or guardians (Lenhart et al., 2010). More than half of teen cell phone users make between one and five calls a day, while the average adult makes and receives about five calls a day (Lenhart et al., 2010).

Perhaps the most crucial distinction between teen adult cell phone users is the question of who pays the bills. While many adults participate in some kind of family plan and many (particularly younger) adults do have a family member or loved one pay for their phone use, by and large adult cell phone users are much more likely to be independent when it comes to purchasing plans, minutes, and data. Seventy percent of teens have phones completely paid for (meaning both the initial phone purchase as well as the monthly plan or contract) by someone else (Lenhart et al., 2010). Once teens have the phone, it's rare that its purchaser takes a hands-off approach, or that parents foot the bill without scrutinizing it or setting limits. Sixty-four percent of parents say that they look at their child's phone—including the contacts, call history, text messages, or photos (Lenhart et al., 2010). Fifty-two percent of parents say they restrict the times of day when their child can use the phone, while 48 percent say they use the phone to monitor their teen's location (either by calling to check up on the teen, or through the use of a GPS-enabled application) (Lenhart et al., 2010).

Although ownership of the phone (or control over its plan) certainly has some hard and fast limits—teens whose parents don't buy a smartphone can't surf the web, while those whose parents employ some kind of lock on texting or calling during specific hours can't participate in these activities unless they tamper with the controls—the question of who pays for the phone and its activities also has some bearing on what teens are *willing* to do with their phones. Teens who pay for the full cost of their phones tend to do more with those phones. Seventy-three percent of teens who pay for their own phone send several texts in a day, compared with 65 percent of teens whose parents pay for their phone (Lenhart et al., 2010). Seventeen percent of teens who pay for their own phones in full report sending sexually suggestive texts, compared with only 3 percent of teens whose parents pay for their phones at least in part (Lenhart, 2009).

While many teens' plans limit their voice minutes—34 percent of teen cell phone users are on a family plan with limited minutes—a full three-quarters of teens (75 percent) are on plans with unlimited texting (Lenhart et al., 2010). Eighteen percent of those teens with unlimited plans report receiving nude or nearly nude images or video via their phones, compared with only 8 percent of those with more limited plans and just 4 percent of teens who pay per message (Lenhart, 2009). Whether teens are afraid of parental monitoring or are simply more likely to engage in risqué behavior when they're sending and receiving texts (or images, or video) on phones that are truly their own, it's clear that financial control of the phone does have some impact on the content teens exchange with one another.

Phones in the Library

Knowing that cell phones and text messages are so ubiquitous in most teens' lives, how do we manage these devices when teens bring them into our library spaces—and how do teens' cell phone habits *outside* the library affect their time spent *inside it*?

Whether you work in a public library or in a school, the decision of whether to allow cell phone use in your space may have already been made for you. If cell phones are banned or allowed only in certain areas, you may find yourself in the uncomfortable position of upholding (or ignoring) rules with which you don't entirely agree. When teachers bring classes to use your computers or access other library resources, whose phone rules apply—the teacher's, or yours? When teens are in the teen section, who decides whether they can use cell phones—the adult reference librarian, or you? Or are any of these spaces policed by rules that were actually created by teens themselves?

It's vital that you know the electronic device policies for your building, whether you work in a public library or a school. Schools often put these policies in the student/parent handbook (although many may also have policies regulating electronic device use by faculty and staff on school property or during school hours, which may appear in the faculty/staff handbook, the school committee policies, or even the teacher contract), and many require students and parents to agree to uphold the school's policies before they can access school-owned technology. (We'll discuss this a little later when we get into computers and Internet use.) In public libraries these policies should be accessible to the public in some manner, but they may live in a procedures manual covering *all* aspects of library policy. Patrons may not necessarily sign off on the electronic device policy explicitly, although when they obtain a library card they may sign a general agreement to comply with all rules and procedures.

If your institution's policy is in any way unclear—perhaps one that doesn't outright ban devices but limits them to use during "appropriate times," or one that leaves individual classroom rules up to the discretion of each teacher—or if you're having trouble finding it, talk to your supervisor or principal immediately. Questions to consider:

- When a teacher brings students or classes to the library, whose discretion trumps?
- Who determines whether a time is "appropriate"?
- Do study halls, lunches, passing periods, free blocks, or before and after school fall under the same rules as standard instructional time?
- Can I designate a part of the library or a time of day when cell phone use is allowed?
- Are texting, accessing the web, listening to music, or using apps regulated the same way that phone calls are?

If you have the autonomy to create (or even shape) the rules for your library or your section of the library, strongly consider getting teen input on these rules, either from a formal teen advisory group, student council or other teen leadership organizations, or the input of the teens you see every day. Here are some considerations for you and your teens to keep in mind:

- **Teens aren't the only ones who use your space.** If your library has no distinct teen area, teen patrons may be using the same space and resources as adult patrons and children. Remind them that what is appropriate for them and their peers may not be appropriate for younger children, and that what they consider normal volume levels or social activity may be disruptive to other patrons.
- **Not all phone features are alike.** Teens may understand that a loud phone conversation would annoy someone trying to read or work, but not realize that the volume is up so high on a song or app that bystanders can hear even with headphones. Texting may seem like a more discreet activity, but it can be rude and distracting while someone else is speaking or a program is underway. One of my personal pet peeves is the student who starts to ask a question about a book or database, then pauses to answer a call or text.
- **Everyone in the library doesn't have the same agenda.** No matter the type of library, all the patrons who happen to be in the room at the same time aren't necessarily sharing the same goals. Some are doing research or homework. Some are doing leisure reading, filling out the crossword, or downloading a new game. Others are simply killing time or looking for friends to talk to about a class or this weekend's plans. Even if a teen protests that "no one cares" if they listen to music loudly or talk on the phone, remember that some patrons—including teens—are too afraid of social retribution to complain about distracting or disruptive behavior from others. I've had students approach me during study hall and ask if I would reprimand another student, but wait until they had sat back down to do it so that the disruptive students wouldn't know who had complained.

Beyond the question of what teens do on their phones while they're in the library or at school, there's the question of how much bearing their outside phone use has on their (and your) activities in the library. If you work in a public library, there's very little chance you or a coworker will be confiscating personal electronic devices; more likely you would ask a patron to leave after a certain number of offenses. In schools, however, teachers and administrators may follow procedures that allow them to confiscate, and even search, students' phones.

New Jersey vs. T.L.O. (1985) established that school searches of student property must be justified from the outset and limited to the scope of investigating the initial (alleged) rule violation or illegal activity that prompted the search in the first place. (The original case involved a student accused of smoking in a lavatory; her purse was searched and when cigarettes were removed from it—even though *possession* of tobacco products was not a violation of the school's rules or state law at the time—an assistant vice principal discovered evidence of marijuana use, a much more serious rule and legal infraction.) This means that if school officials have reasonable justification to search a student's bag or locker, they can only search texts or other contents of a cell phone for evidence of that same infraction. The ACLU of Northern California, however, in a study of 164 school districts, found that the overwhelming majority of districts (101, or about 62 percent) only required reasonable suspicion for a search, with no guidelines or recommendation on the scope of search (Hamme and Villagra, 2011).

Indeed, the ACLU raises a number of privacy issues that should alarm anyone who works with teens. Administrators who search teens' phones could find evidence of their sexuality or gender identity that may be a secret from peers or family members. Although not all cases have explicitly involved cell phones or other technology, teachers and administrators across the country have outed teens; a Florida student who told her principal she had been taunted by younger students for being a lesbian left the office in tears after he demanded her parents' phone number to inform them she was gay, told her that homosexuality was wrong, and threatened her with suspension if she went near her abusers again (*Gillman v. School Board for Holmes County, Florida*, 2008). These kinds of searches could also reveal the political beliefs, financial situations, personal or romantic relationships, or even medical details of the teen in question (not to mention any friends or family members they may have conversed with), none of which may be relevant to the investigation at hand (Hamme and Villagra, 2011). The ACLU has documented numerous cases where school officials illegally searched students' phones, including a Colorado administrator who impersonated a student using his seized cell phone (ACLU of Colorado, 2007) and a Pennsylvania principal who punished a student for possessing "explicit" photographs of herself on her own phone (ACLU, 2010).

Even though you may not be the adult who will confiscate the phone or dole out consequences of rule-breaking behavior, you can be an ally to your teens. When you see a phone confiscated, tell your administrator exactly what you saw. If you see another adult expanding a phone search beyond the scope of the original complaint, ask what these other texts or photos have to do with the matter at hand. Ask if a parent or guardian can be present before a search takes place, or even a trusted teacher or advisor (particularly if you know an LGBTQ student would want backup from a supportive adult).

Teens may also voluntarily bring their phones to *you*, to document cyberbullying or harassment. *Even if they physically hand a phone over to you*, it's vital that you ask for permission before you view anything else on the phone; even better, hand the phone back and ask them to walk you through the rest of the conversation. A single text message or photo may seem inflammatory, but reading or viewing others in context will give you a better idea of the situation (and help the teen see how their own words or actions may have played a part in the conflict). If you've seen or read something that worries you, be up front with the teen: "I really appreciate that you trusted me enough to show me this, but I'm worried this situation could get out of hand. Can we talk about this together with [a coworker, a parent or family member, law enforcement]?" If a teen shows you evidence that he or she or someone the teen knows has harmed someone or is in danger of harming someone or of self-harm, you can't be the last adult to get this information. "I'm so glad you told me about this because we need to get help. Can we both go talk to someone who will help make sure this doesn't happen again?"

Teens and Social Networks

Fully 95 percent of all teens ages 12–17 are now online, and 80 percent of those teens are members of a social network (Lenhart et al., 2011). Social media spaces aren't vacuums, and they aren't entirely separate from teens' face-to-face interactions. They mirror traditional social spaces in some ways, and amplify the interactions and reactions that take place there in other ways. Just like adults, teens use online spaces to escape, to explore, to experiment, and to participate in the evolving world around them.

For the vast majority of teen social media users, online social life boils down to either Facebook or Facebook and another tool/network. Account ownership breaks down like this:

- Facebook: 93 percent
- MySpace: 24 percent
- Twitter: 12 percent
- Yahoo: 7 percent
- YouTube: 6 percent
- Skype, myYearbook, and Tumblr: 2 percent each
- Google Buzz: 1 percent (Lenhart et al., 2011)

Membership (or active membership) in some of these spaces does differ somewhat by age, gender, and race. Girls are twice as likely to use Twitter as boys (22 percent of online girls tweet, compared with 10 percent of online boys), and black teens are three times as likely to tweet than either white or Latino teens (fully one-third of online black teens use Twitter) (Lenhart et al., 2011). It's also noteworthy that Twitter usage among teens has skyrocketed in the past two years, doubling from 2009. This means that teens and adults now use Twitter at about the same rate, with Twitter users representing 12 percent of online adults (Lenhart et al., 2011). Though MySpace usage has dropped overall, 35 percent of Latino teen social media users have a MySpace account, compared with only 22 percent of white teens. Additionally, 32 percent of teen social media users whose parents did not go to college have a MySpace account, compared with 18 percent of those whose parents attended at least some college (Lenhart et al., 2011).

Privacy, safety, and the ramifications of what teens do online are clearly on the minds of many parents. Ninety-four percent of parents of online teens say they have talked with their teen about what should and shouldn't be shared online, 93 percent have talked about ways to use the Internet safely, and 87 percent have made suggestions about how to behave online and what their children do (or don't do) on the Internet (Lenhart et al., 2011). Eighty percent of parents who use social media (and who have social media–using children) have friended their child online—translating into 45 percent of all online parents of teens and 39 percent of all parents of teens overall who are "friends" with their children online. Seventy-seven percent have checked which websites their child visited, up from 65 percent who did in 2006. Sixty-six percent have searched to find what information was available about their child online. Interestingly, only 61 percent of teens report that their parents have checked their social networking profile. About half of parents still use parental controls to influence their child's online activities, including 54 percent who use some means of blocking, filtering, or monitoring. Parents who are friends with their child online are more likely to use parental controls, while teens who are friends with their parents online are more likely to report that an experience with social media caused a problem with their parents (Lenhart et al., 2011).

More than two-thirds of social media–using teens believe that their peers are mostly kind to one another on social networking sites, while 20 percent think their peers are mostly unkind. Among adults 18 and older, on the other hand, a full 85 percent reported that people are mostly kind, while only 5 percent believed people were mostly unkind (Lenhart et al., 2011). Eighty-eight percent of social media–using teens have seen other people being mean or cruel on social networks, compared with 69 percent of adults. Interesting, adults and teens are just about as likely to say that someone has been mean or cruel to *them personally* online in the past year—15 percent of teens and 13 percent of adults (Lenhart et al., 2011).

We see no significant difference in the rates of online cruelty experienced *directly*— teens who say someone has been cruel or mean to *them*—by older teens versus younger teens, girls versus boys, or teens from higher- or lower-income families. Younger girls (ages 12 to 13) are more likely to say that their experience online has been mostly unkind; however, one in three younger teen girls who are social media users says that her peers are mostly unkind to one another online. Although 72 percent of white and 78 percent of Latino youth say that people are mostly kind on social networking sites, only 56 percent of black teens say the same (Lenhart et al., 2011).

Despite the prevalence of cyberbullying in the media, it's important to note that online bullying rates are still lower than bullying in person. Twelve percent of teens report being bullied in person in the past year, while 8 percent say they've experienced some kind of online bullying—whether through e-mail, social networking cites, or instant messaging. Except in person, where boys and girls report bullying in more or less equal numbers, girls are much more likely to report bullying by other methods— online, by phone, or by text message (Lenhart et al., 2011).

Do you know how many of the teens who use your library go online to participate in social networks? Do you know whether they use customized privacy settings, whether they've hidden their information from teachers and other adults, or whether they use social networks for school projects? Do you have difficulty keeping the peace between teens who want to watch YouTube videos and peruse one another's Facebook walls and the patrons—teens as well as adults—who want to fill out job applications, do research, and write their college essays? Does your school or library have an online presence? Would you let a teen "friend" you? These are the questions facing those of us who work with teens, and none of them have easy answers.

Social Networks and Library Computers

Again, if you work in a school, the decision about whether or not to allow Facebook access on library computers may have been decided for you. Many schools still block a wide variety of sites—from Facebook and Twitter to Tumblr and gaming sites— that they aren't specifically required to block by law. Under the Children's Internet Protection Act (CIPA), a "federal law enacted by Congress to address concerns about access to offensive content over the Internet on school and library computers," any school or library receiving E-Rate funding for Internet access or internal connections has to do the following:

- Block or filter Internet access to images that are obscene, qualify as child pornography, or are harmful to minors (on any computers that might be accessed by minors).
- Adopt and enforce a policy to monitor the online activities of minors.
- Adopt and implement an Internet safety policy that addresses minors' access to inappropriate online material, minors' safety and security when using online communications, hacking and other illegal activities by minors, unauthorized use or distributions of minors' personal information, and measures restricting minors' access to harmful materials. (Federal Communications Commission, 2012)

Whew—quite a mouthful, and quite controversial in many circles. What qualifies as "harmful to minors"? CIPA doesn't require the tracking of minors' Internet use, but otherwise how do we "monitor" their online activities? And what if the same filters intended to block access to pornography and alcohol also filter out legitimate websites that have no harmful content? You'll also notice that CIPA has no mention of Facebook or other social networking sites, yet these are still routinely blocked in many schools and districts across the country.

If Facebook is currently blocked in your school or library, ask why. More and more teens are finding that Facebook can be used as a social network, yes, but also as an *educational* network. Many schools and students use Facebook to communicate to entire classes, to promote the yearbook or other school publications, to send work on group projects to one another, to post school announcements, or to promote an athletic program. Why should these activities be blocked in the school building? Additionally, if schools and districts enact policies forbidding faculty from interacting with students on social networks, this ensures that teachers are shut out from a social realm where students are *already living their educational lives*—and are often accessing it during school hours anyway by bypassing "security" measures.

If the rationale for blocking Facebook is the distraction it may pose during classes, ask if the ban must be a blanket one. Does it apply before and after school? During lunch? In study hall or a free period? What if a student has finished all of his or her work during a period? Can a teacher lift the block on an individual terminal, or can a librarian allow one lab to be open to students doing independent work while a class works in the other (with games and social networks blocked)? In other words, can the blocking of these sites be at the discretion of an individual teacher or faculty member?

In a public library setting, you may be less likely to have a ban on social networks (although the computers will likely still be filtered for pornography), but you may still have to navigate the politics of such a ban when other patrons (particularly if adult patrons share computers with teens) complain that they want to do something "productive" and all the computers are in use by teens instant-messaging and surfing Facebook. What's your policy on computer use? Are terminals strictly used on a timed basis, or do you recognize any hierarchy of "productivity?" How would you define it? Ask your teens: How would you feel if you needed to write an essay and all the computers were being used, but you could see that someone was on Facebook? Would you assume they were just goofing off? Would you think you had a right to a computer because you'd be doing schoolwork? What if you had a few tabs open and you were switching back and forth between Facebook, e-mail, and your essay? Are you still using the computer in an appropriate way?

If teens don't have access to Facebook and other social networks on your library computers, they're no doubt still accessing it—from outside the building, from their phones and other mobile devices that don't have to access the school's network, and by circumventing the school's filters. (A surprising number of school filters, particularly if your district is still using an outdated version of the software purchased years ago, can be easily fooled by using https:// instead of http:// in front of URLs.) Their online interactions are bound to bleed into their interactions at the school and the library.

Sometimes it's obvious when teens are clashing over things said or done online. I've found forgotten printouts of Facebook pages, lengthy Formspring threads, even whole instant-messaging conversations. Sometimes teens print these to bring to an administrator as evidence of cyberbullying, or intend to print out unflattering photographs to (not-so-)surreptitiously post around the building, or just to share with friends (and pore over endlessly for meaning, much the same way teens used to compare handwritten notes and letters). Other times you may notice a group of teens all flocked around a single phone or monitor, having an animated discussion about someone's Facebook wall or reading messages intended to be private. But as with face-to-face bullying, cyberbullying situations can make it very difficult to distinguish bully from victim.

Just as teens' real-world social circles evolve from day to day—even from hour to hour—their online social communities reflect these rapid changes, sometimes amplifying them. The anonymity that the Internet affords, even in spheres such as Facebook where comments and messages are explicitly linked to a nameable persona, can lead teens (and adults) to take risks and use language that they may not ordinarily use in person. Coupled with the difficulty that written language poses in conveying the full emotion of a face-to-face interaction (which is usually supplemented by body language, tone, and other context markers), this anonymity can rapidly escalate online encounters—which then spill into the social world of teens' face-to-face lives.

If the teens you serve are experiencing conflict over online interactions, here are some questions you can ask to help them think about the ways their virtual conflicts are affecting their lives:

- How can you be sure that a text message or e-mail is really coming from the person you think it is?
- Do you ever leave your laptop or phone unattended while you're logged in to Facebook or another social network?
- Do you think an IM exchange is the same as a face-to-face conversation? Why not?
- Are there some topics you think should be discussed face-to-face? Would you feel better or worse if someone broke up with you online? What about inviting you to a social event?
- How many friends do you have online? Do you count them as "real" friends? Do you feel as close or closer to them as your in-person friends?
- Have you ever "said" something online that you wouldn't say to someone in person?
- How do you feel when you see someone being mean to someone you know online?

Stories involving cell phones, the Internet, and crimes get sensational amounts of media attention, but ultimately all the behaviors that teens carry out in their virtual lives can also take place in the "real" world. It's up to us as adults to help teens recognize the same negative patterns of traditional teen social life that pop up in their virtual spaces, and support them when they're having difficulty navigating *any* social spaces.

References

ACLU (American Civil Liberties Union). 2010. "ACLU Settles Student-Cell-Phone-Search Lawsuit with Northeast Pennsylvania School District." ACLU. http://www.aclu.org/free-speech/aclu-settles-student-cell-phone-search-lawsuit-northeast-pennsylvania-school-district.

ACLU (American Civil Liberties Union) of Colorado. 2007. "School Administrators Violate Colorado Law, Constitutional Rights by Searching Students' Text Messages." ACLU of Colorado. http://aclu-co.org/news/school-administrators-violate-colorado-law-constitutional-rights-by-searching-students-text-mes.

Federal Communications Commission. 2012. "Children's Internet Protection Act." Federal Communications Commission. Accessed April 25. http://www.fcc.gov/guides/childrens-internet-protection-act.

Gillman vs. School Board for Holmes County, Florida, 567 F. Supp. 2d 1359 (2008).

Hamme, Brendan, and Hector O. Villagra. 2011. "Hello! Students Have a Right to Privacy in Their Cell Phones: Indiscriminate Cell Phone Searches Violent Students' Privacy Rights." ACLU of Northern California. http://www.aclunc.org/issues/youth/asset_upload_file124_10547.

Lenhart, Amanda. 2009. "Teens and Sexting." Pew Internet & American Life Project. December 15. http://www.pewinternet.org/Reports/2009/Teens-and-Sexting.aspx.

———. 2010. "Cell Phones and American Adults." Pew Internet & American Life Project. September 2. http://www.pewinternet.org/Reports/2010/Cell-Phones-and-American-Adults.aspx.

Lenhart, Amanda, Rich Ling, Scott Campbell, and Kristen Purcell. 2010. "Teens and Mobile Phones." Pew Internet & American Life Project. April 20. http://www.pewinternet.org/Reports/2010/Teens-and-Mobile-Phones.aspx.

Lenhart, Amanda, Mary Madden, Aaron Smith, Kristen Purcell, Kathryn Zickuhr, and Lee Rainie. 2011. "Teens, Kindness and Cruelty on Social Network Sites." Pew Internet & American Life Project. November 9. http://www.pewinternet.org/Reports/2011/Teens-and-social-media/Summary.aspx.

New Jersey vs. T.L.O., 469 U.S. 325 (1985).

Bibliography

ACLU (American Civil Liberties Union). 2010. "ACLU Settles Student-Cell-Phone-Search Lawsuit with Northeast Pennsylvania School District." ACLU. http://www.aclu.org/free-speech/aclu-settles-student-cell-phone-search-lawsuit-northeast-pennsylvania-school-district.

———. 2011. "Don't Filter Me: Web Content Filtering in Schools." ACLU. Accessed July 7. http://www.aclu.org/dont-filter-me-web-content-filtering-schools.

ACLU (American Civil Liberties Union) of Colorado. 2007. "School Administrators Violate Colorado Law, Constitutional Rights by Searching Students' Text Messages." ACLU of Colorado. http://aclu-co.org/news/ school-administrators-violate-colorado-law-constitutional-rights-by-searching-students-text-mes.

American Academy of Child and Adolescent Psychiatry. 2010. "Alcohol and Drug Abuse." American Academy of Child and Adolescent Psychiatry. Accessed September 16, 2011. http://www.aacap.org/cs/root/resources_for_families/glossary_of_symptoms_and_ illnesses/alcohol_and_drug_abuse.

———. 2011. "Teens: Alcohol and Other Drugs." American Academy of Child and Adolescent Psychiatry. Updated March. http://www.aacap.org/cs/root/facts_for_families/teens_alcohol_and_other_drugs.

American Academy of Pediatrics. 2011. "Critical Adolescent Health Issues—Mental Health and Substance Abuse." American Academy of Pediatrics. Accessed September 16. http://www.aap.org/sections/adolescenthealth/mentalhealth.cfm.

American Psychiatric Association. 2000. *Diagnostic and Statistical Manual of Mental Disorders* (4th ed., text rev.). Washington, DC: American Psychiatric Association.

Americans with Disabilities Act of 1990, as Amended. 2008. United States Code (P.L. 101–336, July 26, 1990). http://www.ada.gov/pubs/adastatute08.htm#subchapterI.

Arciaga, Michelle, Wayne Sakamoto, and Errika Fearbry Jones. 2010. "Responding to Gangs in the School Setting." National Gang Center. http://www.nationalgangcenter.gov/Content/Documents/Bulletin-5.pdf.

Brame, Robert, Michael C. Turner, Raymond Paternoster, and Shawn D. Bushway. 2012. "Cumulative Prevalence of Arrest from Ages 8 to 23 in a National Sample." *Pediatrics* 129, no. 1: 21–28.

Break the Cycle. 2009. "Dating Violence 101." Break the Cycle. Accessed August 28, 2011. http://www.breakthecycle.org/dating-violence-101.

Brown, Jennifer. 2011. *Bitter End*. New York: Little, Brown and Company.

Centers for Disease Control and Prevention. 2011a. "Leading Causes of Death." Centers for Disease Control and Prevention. http://www.cdc.gov/nchs/fastats/lcod.htm.

———. 2011b. "Smoking." Centers for Disease Control and Prevention. http://www.cdc.gov/nchs/fastats/smoking.htm.

———. 2011c. "Teen Birth Rates Declined Again in 2009." Centers for Disease Control and Prevention. Last updated July 1. http://www.cdc.gov/features/dsTeenPregnancy/.

———. 2012. "Understanding Teen Dating Violence." Centers for Disease Control and Prevention. http://www.cdc.gov/ViolencePrevention/pdf/TeenDatingViolence2012-a.pdf.

Coalition for Juvenile Justice. 2011a. "2011 Federal Funding Fact Sheet." Coalition for Juvenile Justice. Accessed September 21. http://www.juvjustice.org/media/factsheets/factsheet_15.pdf.

———. 2011b. "Conditions of Confinement for Young Offenders." Coalition for Juvenile Justice. Accessed September 21. http://www.juvjustice.org/media/factsheets/factsheet_4.pdf.

———. 2011c. "Ensuring School Engagement and Success vs. Exclusion for Youth at Risk of Delinquency." Accessed September 21. http://www.juvjustice.org/media/factsheets/factsheet_11.pdf.

———. 2011d. "Mental Health Needs of Youth and Young Offenders." Coalition for Juvenile Justice. Accessed September 21. http://www.juvjustice.org/media/factsheets/factsheet_8.pdf.

———. 2011e. "Prevention: Saving Lives and Dollars." Coalition for Juvenile Justice. Accessed September 21. http://www.juvjustice.org/media/factsheets/factsheet_9.pdf.

Covenant House Institute. 2010. "A National Picture of Youth Homelessness." Covenant House. http://www.covenanthouse.org/sites/default/files/National%20Picture%20of%20Youth%20Homelessness%2010.14.10.pdf.

Eisenberg. Marla E., Linda H. Bearinger, Renee E. Sieving, Carolyne Swain, and Michael D. Resnick. 2004. "Parents' Beliefs about Condoms and Oral Contraceptives: Are They Medically Accurate?" *Perspectives on Sexual and Reproductive Health* 36, no. 2. Guttmacher Institute. http://www.guttmacher.org/pubs/journals/3605004.html.

Federal Communications Commission. 2012. "Children's Internet Protection Act." Federal Communications Commission. Accessed April 25. http://www.fcc.gov/guides/childrens-internet-protection-act.

Feliz, Josie. 2011. "National Study Confirms Teen Drug Use Trending in Wrong Direction: Marijuana, Ecstasy Use Up Since 2008, Parents Feel Ill-Equipped to Respond." The Partnership at Drugfree.org. April 6. http://www.drugfree.org/newsroom/national-study-confirms-teen-drug-use-trending-in-wrong-direction-marijuana-ecstasy-use-up-since-2008-parents-feel-ill-equipped-to-respond.

Ford-Martin, Paula Anne, Teresa G. Odle, and Tish Davidson. 2009a. "Bipolar Disorder." In *The Gale Encyclopedia of Medicine*, edited by Jacqueline L. Longe. Detroit: Gale.

———. 2009b. "Depression." In *The Gale Encyclopedia of Medicine*, edited by Jacqueline L. Longe. Detroit: Gale.

Gay, Kathleen, and Whittington, Christine. 2002. *Body Marks: Tattooing, Piercing, and Scarification*. Brookfield, CT: Twenty-First Century Books.

Gillman vs. School Board for Holmes County, Florida, 567 F. Supp. 2d 1359 (2008).

GLSEN (Gay, Lesbian and Straight Education Network). 2012. "Safe Space Kit." Accessed July 7, 2011. http://www.glsen.org/cgi-bin/iowa/all/news/record/1641.html.

Guttmacher Institute. 2012a. "Facts on American Teens' Sexual and Reproductive Health." Guttmacher Institute. February. http://www.guttmacher.org/pubs/FB-ATSRH.html.

———. 2012b. "Facts on American Teens' Sources of Information about Sex." Guttmacher Institute. February. http://www.guttmacher.org/pubs/FB-Teen-Sex-Ed.html.

H. Lee Moffitt Cancer Center and Research Institute. 2000. "Forever Free, Booklet 3—A Guide to Remaining Smoke Free: Smoking and Weight." H. Lee Moffitt Cancer Center and Research Institute at the University of South Florida. Accessed September 19, 2011. http://www.smokefree.gov/pubs/ffree3.pdf.

Hamme, Brendan, and Hector O. Villagra. 2011. "Hello! Students Have a Right to Privacy in Their Cell Phones: Indiscriminate Cell Phone Searches Violent Students' Privacy Rights." ACLU of Northern California. http://www.aclunc.org/issues/youth/asset_upload_file124_10547.

Hardy, Lal, ed. 2009. *The Mammoth Book of Tattoos*. Philadelphia: Running Press.

Hasler, Nikol. 2010. *Sex: A Book for Teens: An Uncensored Guide to Your Body, Sex, and Safety*. San Francisco: Zest Books.

HUD (U.S. Department of Housing and Urban Development). 2011. "Homeless Emergency Assistance and Rapid Transition to Housing: Defining Homeless, Final Rule." *Federal Register* 76 (December 5): 75995–75997. http://www.hudhre.info/documents/HEARTH_HomelessDefinition_FinalRule.pdf.

Irish, Lora S. 2007. *Great Book of Tattoo Designs*. East Petersburg, PA: Fox Chapel.

Jones, Rachel K., and Biddlecom, Ann E. 2011. "Is the Internet Filling the Sexual Health Information Gap for Teens? An Exploratory Study." *Journal of Health Communication: International Perspectives* 16, no. 2. http://www.tandfonline.com/doi/abs/10.1080/10810730.2010.535112.

Lenhart, Amanda. 2009. "Teens and Sexting." Pew Internet & American Life Project. December 15. http://www.pewinternet.org/Reports/2009/Teens-and-Sexting.aspx.

———. 2010. "Cell Phones and American Adults." Pew Internet & American Life Project. September 2. http://www.pewinternet.org/Reports/2010/Cell-Phones-and-American-Adults.aspx.

Lenhart, Amanda, Rich Ling, Scott Campbell, and Kristen Purcell. 2010. "Teens and Mobile Phones." Pew Internet & American Life Project. April 20. http://www.pewinternet.org/Reports/2010/Teens-and-Mobile-Phones.aspx.

Lenhart, Amanda, Mary Madden, Aaron Smith, Kristen Purcell, Kathryn Zickuhr, and Lee Rainie. 2011. "Teens, Kindness and Cruelty on Social Network Sites." Pew Internet & American Life Project. November 9. http://www.pewinternet.org/Reports/2011/Teens-and-social-media/Summary.aspx.

Levy, Janey. 2009. *Tattooing: Tattoos in Modern Society*. New York: The Rosen Publishing Group.

Liz Claiborne, Inc. 2007. "Tech Abuse in Teen Relationships Study." LoveIsRespect.org. http://www.loveisrespect.org/wp-content/uploads/2009/03/liz-claiborne-2007-tech-relationship-abuse.pdf.

———. 2008. "Teen and Tween Dating Violence and Abuse Study." LoveIsRespect.org. http://www.loveisrespect.org/wp-content/uploads/2008/07/tru-tween-teen-study-feb-081 .pdf.

Mayo Clinic Staff. 2010a. "Piercings: How to Prevent Complications." Mayo Clinic. February 16. http://www.mayoclinic.com/health/piercings/SN00049.

———. 2010b. "Tattoos: Understand Risks and Precautions." Mayo Clinic. February 16. http://www.mayoclinic.com/health/tattoos-and-piercings/MC00020.

Mental Health America. 2007. "Position Statement 31: Employment Development of Services for Adults in Recovery for Mental Illness." Mental Health America. June 10. http://www .nmha.org/go/position-statements/31.

National Center for Chronic Disease Prevention and Health Promotion. 2010a. "Alcohol & Drug Use." Centers for Disease Control and Prevention. Last modified June 3. http://www.cdc.gov/healthyyouth/alcoholdrug/index.htm.

———. 2010b. "Tobacco Use and the Health of Young People." Centers for Disease Control and Prevention. Last modified June 3. http://www.cdc.gov/healthyyouth/tobacco/facts.htm.

National Center on Addiction and Substance Abuse at Columbia University. 2010. "National Survey of American Attitudes on Substance Abuse XV: Teens and Parents." Columbia University. http://www.casacolumbia.org/upload/2010/20100819teensurvey.pdf.

National Coalition for the Homeless. 2008. "Homeless Youth." National Coalition for the Homeless. June. http://www.nationalhomeless.org/factsheets/youth.html.

———. 2009. "How Many People Experience Homelessness?" National Coalition for the Homeless. July. http://www.nationalhomeless.org/factsheets/How_Many.html.

National Institute of Mental Health. 2011a. "Anxiety Disorders in Children and Adolescents (Fact Sheet)." National Institutes of Health. Last reviewed April 29. http://nimh.nih.gov/ health/publications/anxiety-disorders-in-children-and-adolescents/index.shtml.

———. 2011b. "Any Disorder among Adults." National Institutes of Health. Accessed September 20. http://nimh.nih.gov/statistics/1ANYDIS_ADULT.shtml.

———. 2011c. "Depression in Children and Adolescents (Fact Sheet)." National Institutes of Health. Last reviewed April 25. http://nimh.nih.gov/health/publications/depression-in-children-and-adolescents/index.shtml.

———. 2012. "Bipolar Disorder in Children and Adolescents (Fact Sheet)." National Institutes of Health. Last reviewed February 13. http://nimh.nih.gov/health/publications/bipolar-disorder-in-children-and-adolescents/index.shtml.

National Institute on Drug Abuse. 2011. "Commonly Abused Drugs Chart." National Institutes of Health. Accessed September 19. http://www.nida.nih.gov/DrugPages/DrugsofAbuse .html.

New Jersey vs. T.L.O., 469 U.S. 325 (1985).

Office of Juvenile Justice and Delinquency Prevention. 2010. "Statistical Briefing Book." U.S. Department of Justice, Office of Justice Programs. http://www.ojjdp.gov/ojstatbb/default .asp.

Quintana, Nico Sifra, Josh Rosenthal, and Jeff Krehely. 2010. "On the Streets: The Federal Response to Gay and Transgender Homeless Youth." Center for American Progress. June. http://www.americanprogress.org/issues/2010/06/pdf/lgbtyouthhomelessness.pdf.

Redd, Nancy Amanda. 2008. *Body Drama*. New York: Gotham.

Santelli, John S., Laura Duberstein Lindberg, Lawrence B. Finer, and Susheela Singh. 2007. "Explaining Recent Declines in Adolescent Pregnancy in the United States: The Contribution of Abstinence and Improved Contraceptive Use." *The American Journal of Public Health* 97, no. 1. http://www.ncbi.nlm.nih.gov/pmc/articles/PMC1716232/.

Search Institute. 2011a. "About Us." Search Institute. Accessed July 4. http://www.search-institute.org/about.

———. 2011b. "What Kids Need: The Building Blocks for Children and Youth." Search Institute. Accessed July 4. http://www.search-institute.org/developmental-assets.

Sex Work Awareness. 2011. "Sex and the Library: A Research Study on Sexuality Information Access in U.S. Public Libraries." Sexuality Information Access in U.S. Public Libraries. Accessed July 7. http://www.infoandthelibrary.org/.

Steinberg, Laurence. 2011. "Demystifying the Adolescent Brain." *Educational Leadership* 68, no. 7: 42–46.

Superior Tattoo. 2009. *Tattoo Bible: Book One*. Stillwater, MN: ArtKulture.

———. 2010. *Tattoo Bible: Book Two*. Stillwater, MN: ArtKulture.

U.S. Department of Health and Human Services. 2008. "Attention Deficit Hyperactivity Disorder (ADHD)." http://nimh.nih.gov/health/publications/attention-deficit-hyperactivity-disorder/complete-index.shtml.

U.S. Food and Drug Administration. 2011. "Tattoos & Permanent Makeup." U.S. Department of Health & Human Services. Last updated April 14. http://www.fda.gov/cosmetics/product andingredientsafety/productinformation/ucm108530.htm.

Wienclaw, Ruth A., and Davidson, Tish. 2009. "Anxiety Disorders." In *The Gale Encyclopedia of Medicine*, 3rd ed., edited by Jacqueline L. Longe. Detroit: Gale.

Index

113

About the Author and YALSA

mk Eagle is a transplanted New Englander who can still recite her southern Oregon library card number by heart. She manages the *YALSA Blog* (http://yalsa.ala.org/blog) for the Young Adult Library Services Association and has presented at the ISIS Conference on New Media, Youth & Sexual Health (http://sextech.org/). She is the librarian at Holliston High School (http://libraryhhs.wordpress.com/) and currently resides in Boston with her partner and two ungrateful cats.

The **Young Adult Library Services Association (YALSA)** is the fourth-largest division of the American Library Association, with more than 5,400 members. YALSA's mission is to expand and strengthen library services for teens and young adults. Through its member-driven advocacy, research, and professional development initiatives, YALSA builds the capacity of libraries and librarians to engage, serve, and empower teens and young adults. YALSA's major initiatives include Teen Read Week™ and Teen Tech Week™. Known as the world leader in recommending books and media to those ages 12–18, YALSA each year gives out six literary awards, including the Printz Award, and chooses titles for seven book and media lists. For more information about YALSA, visit http://www.ala.org/yalsa or http://www.ala.org/yalsa/booklists.